THE ULTIMATE HOUSE FLIPPING AND BRRRR REAL ESTATE INVESTING BEGINNER'S BOOK

BUILD WEALTH THROUGH FIX-AND-FLIP AND THE BUY, REHAB, RENT, REFINANCE, REPEAT STRATEGY— EVEN IF YOU'RE ON A TIGHT BUDGET

FRANK EBERSTADT

TABLE OF CONTENTS

Part III

BUILD SMART AND GROW BIG

INTRODUCTION

Financial freedom is the goal, right? I don't think there are many people out there who wouldn't want financial freedom in their lives, where they can say they have built up enough wealth so that finances are not a huge source of stress for them. There are many people who claim to have found the answer to financial freedom with their hacks and business ideas, but the truth is that real estate is one of the most solid investments to ensure financial freedom and wealth building.

Real estate is one of the longest-standing investments available. If you talk to members of the older generation, you will quickly discover that many of them are advocates of investing in real estate. This is because, in general, the return on investment in real estate far outperforms many other traditional investments over the long run. Even though stocks and bonds are good investments, real estate tends to perform better than those. It is one of the most stable, trustworthy, and rewarding investments available.

You might be one of the people who feel that real estate investing is either out of reach or very intimidating. If this is the case, that is okay because you are not alone. We all start somewhere. The truth is, I was definitely apprehensive when it came to real estate investing and whether it was a good option. I only started investing in real estate out of necessity because I needed somewhere to live, and I didn't have much money to pay for it. As a new immigrant family, we didn't have all the resources in the world. The only thing I could afford was an old, broken-down house, but I was willing to put in the work. After a few years of renovating, I refinanced the house, and it was worth much more than I had paid for it. The cash-out I received from refinancing was used to access the equity in my house and put a down payment on a two-bedroom apartment. I used it to start my short-term rental business, and my real estate investment journey began. I know it can be intimidating to start, but I was able to do it, and now I want to help others create the same for themselves.

Before we get ahead of ourselves, let's take some time to define what real estate investing is. Real estate is property that can include land and anything that is permanently attached to or built on it. Typically, real estate is divided into five main categories: commercial, residential, industrial, raw land, and special use land. You can invest in any one of these types, but as a first-time or beginner investor, residential tends to be the better option because it is more accessible and requires less specialized knowledge. When you invest in real estate, you are purchasing the property, land, or home. Then you can either rent or sell the property to make a profit. This is a very simple breakdown of what real estate investing is, as there are many different strategies that fall under this umbrella. The two main strategies we are going to focus on in this book are house flipping and the BRRRR (Buy, Rehab, Rent, Refinance, Repeat) method. We will be diving more into both of these in this book, but let's give you an overview of the BRRRR method. This is a strategy where you buy a property that might need a bit of work and renovate it to increase its value. Then you rent it out for additional income and eventually refinance the property to access equity to fund your next investment property. If this all sounds like another language, don't worry, we are going to cover this and house flipping to help you along your journey. The important thing to know is that both are great strategies to help build your wealth as a beginner real estate investor and see significant gains with your investments.

There are many myths surrounding real estate investing, which discourage a lot of people from even giving it a try. I want to put these myths to rest. You don't need to be wealthy to start investing, nor do you need to be a landlord, own a house, or time the market perfectly. At the end of the day, all you need to do is be willing to start and ensure that you are taking the right steps to reach your goal. While there are risks involved in investing in real estate, the truth is that any investment carries some level of risk. As the saying goes, "no risk, no reward." However, you must do your best to mitigate these risks and ensure that you are not making rushed decisions. It is important to understand that sometimes we need to take a step in the right direction for things to work out. There are numerous success stories of people who started investing in real estate and have now seen significant returns on their investments. You can be one of those success stories, too.

In this book, we will go through a three-part framework that outlines the key elements for investing in real estate through house flipping and the BRRRR method. The first part is the foundational section of the book, where we will learn about the two main strategies we will discuss. Then we will move on to part two, which focuses on taking action and making the right moves to find, fix, rent, or sell the property. The final part, part three, will dive into building smart and growing big. In this section, we will discuss how to grow your investment and ensure that you are making smart decisions to protect yourself and your investment.

My hope for you is that by the end of this book, you will have the confidence to start investing in real estate using your chosen strategy. Both house flipping and the BRRRR method are great ways to begin your real estate investment journey, but it is important to understand what they are and what your first step should be. So, without any further delay, let's dive into Chapter 1, where we will discuss these strategies.

PART I

LEARN THE STRATEGIES

FLIP VS. BRRRR—WHICH ONE'S RIGHT FOR YOU?

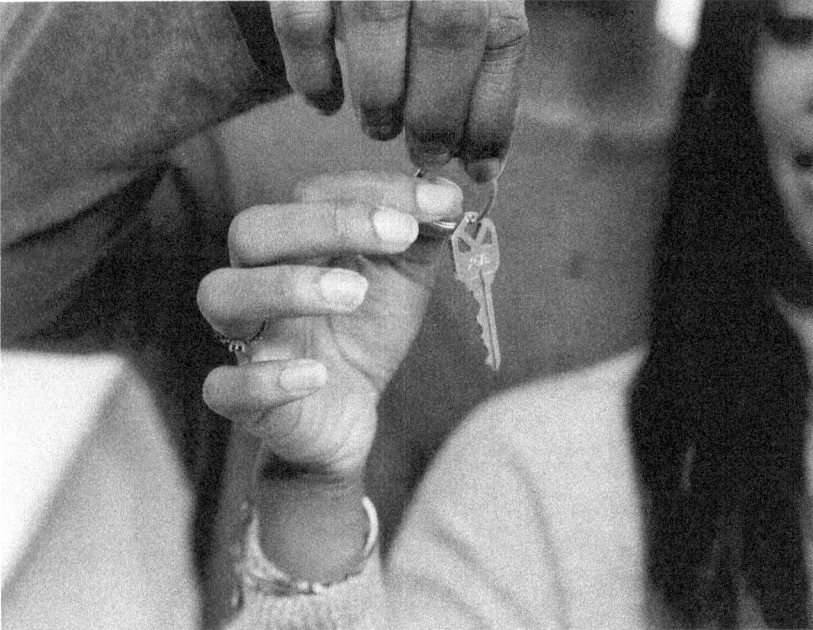

In 2024, the US real estate market saw a notable shift: While traditional home sales faced challenges, investors found opportunities in alternative strategies. Notably, 41% of residential real estate investors reported higher earnings compared to the previous year (Pisano 2024). These figures highlight the potential of informed investment choices.

UNDERSTANDING HOUSE FLIPPING AND THE BRRRR STRATEGY

You may or may not have heard of house flipping before, but I am sure that you have watched a TV show where someone buys houses and renovates them. After the renovations are completed, they sell the house and make a profit. This is the basic principle of house flipping. When someone wants to flip a house, they must conduct extensive research to find a property within a reasonable price range. Then, they will assess what needs to be done to improve the value of the home. This could involve larger projects, such as adding an extra bedroom or bathroom, or removing the entire floor and replacing it with something more modern, durable, and functional. It could also include smaller tasks like repainting, refurnishing, and adding new finishes to the existing amenities and furniture.

Unlike many other real estate investment strategies, when you flip a house, the goal is to make a profit as soon as possible. Remember that a property is a significant investment, and if you are going to put a lot of money into it, you also want to ensure that you can recoup your investment as quickly as possible. Many people who invest in house flipping aim to flip houses frequently so that they can consistently achieve a good return on their investments. If done correctly, flipping houses can be a highly effective investment strategy that yields substantial profits. In fact, in 2024, house flipping generated a median profit of $73,500 per property (Gratton 2025a). That is an impressive return on investment for a strategy that allows you to access your profits relatively quickly after making the investment.

But before you pick up your drill and paintbrush, you need to be aware of the main aspects that lead to house-flipping success. It's not as easy as simply making a property attractive and then selling it off. You will first need to consider the overall market appreciation in the neighborhood where you are going to purchase your property. The truth is that some neighborhoods are better than others when it comes to investing. If a neighborhood has a bad reputation, lacks amenities, or is unsafe or difficult to navigate, then the likelihood of making a good profit is quite slim. People will always prefer to pay a little more to live in a better area, even if the property is smaller than what they would have gotten in a less desirable area.

Another important factor to consider is how much value the improvements will add to the property. You'll need to carefully evaluate which improvements to make based on what will add the most value and, therefore, yield the most profit. Some improvements are merely nice to have; they may enhance the property's appearance or feel, but they do not significantly increase its value when you are trying to resell. Since the goal of property flipping is to maximize profit, it is important to consider which types of renovations and improvements will generate income and which ones may not be worth the investment.

Let's shift gears and discuss something that is often mistaken for house flipping but can be considered a level up from traditional house flipping. It is called the BRRRR method, which stands for Buy, Rehab, Rent, Refinance, and Repeat. The goal is to purchase distressed properties, fix them up, rent them out, and generate income from them. While this is happening, you are building equity, which you can then use toward your next property. Unlike house flipping, you retain possession of the property because you are renting it out for income rather than selling it. This way, it is not a one-time profit but rather a source of income over a longer timeframe.

In order for this method to work, an investor will need to make sure they can make enough money through their rent to cover the mortgage. If they are only able to rent out the property for less than the amount they have to pay on their monthly mortgage payments, it means that they will not be making a profit, and this investment is going to be a losing battle.

In order to almost guarantee that you will make a good profit from this method, you need to ensure that you are purchasing a property at a discounted price. The cheaper you can buy a property, the more potential you have to make a larger profit. With that said, you must conduct thorough research to ensure that the area, as well as other factors, will work in your favor. There is no point in purchasing a property that is cheap if it has absolutely nothing else going for it. We will dive deeper into the BRRRR method in Chapter 5, so stay tuned for an in-depth exploration of the method later in the book.

For now, let's discuss some of the numbers you might expect in a successful BRRRR deal (Blankenship 2023b). Let's say you have a property that you are looking to purchase, and it costs $100,000. The closing costs are $5,000, with the rehab costs being around $25,000. All in all, this means that the total cost for which you will need to secure a loan would be $130,000. The monthly rent is $1,200, which means that the annual rent taken in would be $14,400. After you have completed all of the renovations, the new value of the property is $180,000, and your new loan amount, which is 80% of the appraised value, is $144,000. This means your cash pullout would be $14,000.

The new monthly mortgage payment, with a 4% interest rate over 30 years, would be $687. Now you have $14,000 freed up, which you can use as the down payment on another property, allowing you to repeat the BRRRR method. If the monthly mortgage payment is $687 and the monthly rent you will be charging is $1,200, it means that you are making a significant profit that you can reinvest into the mortgage or use to finance another property, depending on what works best for you. This is how the BRRRR method operates in real life.

PROS AND CONS

As you can probably tell, there are some definite similarities between house flipping and the BRRRR method. While those similarities are important, it is even more crucial to note the differences when deciding which method you will use to build your property investment portfolio. Both strategies start by acquiring an undervalued property and then renovating it to increase its value. The difference lies in the exit strategy: House flipping focuses on selling the property as quickly as possible to make a profit, while the BRRRR method emphasizes renting out the property and creating equity so you can continue investing.

House Flipping

Pros

With house flipping, there are plenty of pros that make it attractive to many investors. One of the most appealing aspects is the potential for a quick profit. When a house flip is done correctly, you can achieve faster returns on your investment compared to most other real estate strategies. Once your house is on the market and sold, you will receive almost immediate profits from it. The goal of house flipping is to renovate and sell the house as soon as possible to secure these quick profits. Additionally, as a house flipper, you will be improving a property's value through upgrades and renovations, allowing you to see the value you are creating on the property as it unfolds.

You will also begin to gain a wealth of market knowledge simply by the nature of house flipping. You will be buying and selling properties quite often, which means you will develop a better understanding of the real estate market in your local area. This knowledge is invaluable as you continue your real estate investment journey. If you are investing in real estate in other ways, choosing house flipping can be a great way to diversify your current portfolio. You can expand your portfolio and increase your potential profit by engaging in something a little different and more hands-on.

Cons

One of the biggest potential downsides to house flipping is the risk of significant financial losses due to unforeseen problems or inadequate research conducted prior to purchasing the property. When it comes to any form of real estate investing, some risk is always involved; therefore, it is crucial to understand what you are getting into before you jump in. Additionally, house flipping is resource- and time-intensive, which means it requires a considerable amount of work as well as a substantial financial investment.

In addition to the money and resources needed to complete a house-flipping project, you must also consider the time commitment and the potential stress of the process. As an investor, you will need to be present every step of the way as the property undergoes renovation. This is essential to ensure that everything runs smoothly, and if any issues arise, you will need to be there to address them to achieve the desired outcome. If you have ever undertaken any building project, you know that unexpected challenges can arise, and many aspects may not go according to plan. This can be highly stressful and may require more resources, time, and money than you initially anticipated. This is why it is so important to be resilient in your thinking and quick on your feet when choosing to invest in this manner.

BRRRR Method

Pros

With this method, there are numerous advantages that make investing in this way very attractive to many investors. One of the biggest draws is simply that you have access to leverage, allowing you to withdraw a significant portion of your initial investment to invest in another property. This way, you are using your current investment to fund your next investment without actually using your own physical money. Additionally, this approach allows for more cash flow than many other investment opportunities, including the house-flipping method.

Another significant benefit is that you are enabling yourself to build equity through the natural appreciation and value of the property while renting it out. This is because you maintain ownership of the property for a longer period than you would with house flipping. There are also considerable tax benefits associated with owning a rental property, which can certainly be a positive aspect. Finally, there is the advantage of being able to expand and grow your real estate investment portfolio, allowing for a more diversified investment strategy that can lead to greater gains and provide some safety for your investments.

Cons

While refinancing a property does create leverage, there are also risks associated with refinancing. Nothing is ever guaranteed; a property appraisal might come in much lower than you expected, which means you may not receive as much money as you had anticipated. This could result in being tied up financially, leaving you without enough funds to invest in your next property right away. Additionally, you must consider that over-leveraging can pose a risk, especially if you are attempting to leverage your current investments recklessly by continuously borrowing without proper research or by trying to make quick money.

One definite negative aspect to consider if you choose the BRRRR method is the fact that you will be managing multiple properties simultaneously. The goal is to refinance and then have enough money to buy another rental property, repeating the process for as long as possible. This means you will have quite a few rental properties to manage, and rental properties are not a passive source of income. You will need to oversee those properties as well as manage your tenants, which could become a full-time job if you do not hire someone else to handle it.

Like any other real estate investment strategy, overall market volatility must be taken into consideration. Even if you have conducted all the necessary research, property values and rental rates are never set in stone. What you expect to gain from your property may not align with what you actually receive.

Finally, another potential drawback to consider is that the BRRRR method adds a level of complexity that exceeds many other property investment strategies. You will constantly be trying to balance buying, rehabbing, renting, and refinancing to keep this investment strategy moving forward. This is not as straightforward as it appears on paper, as there are many moving parts, and your different properties may be at various stages of the process. Balancing everything will require a significant amount of your time and energy, ensuring that you make the right decisions in each area. It is also important to note that the more properties you take on, the more complex the situation will become. Therefore, you will need to decide for yourself when it is a good time to stop and when you can purchase another property and continue the process.

SO, WHICH STRATEGY SUITS YOU BEST?

When it comes to investing in real estate, there are many different goals that people are trying to achieve. It is important to understand what your goals are so that you can make the right choices. Let's discuss some of the most popular investment goals and which type of real estate investment would be best suited for each.

Short-Term Cash Generation

If you are someone who needs a quick turnaround time to get your money out of your investment as soon as possible, then house flipping is a better option. With house flipping, you can expect to see returns within a few months, and it offers a very clear path toward achieving your short-term returns.

Long-Term Wealth Building

If your goal is to build wealth gradually over a longer period, then the BRRRR method of real estate investing is a better choice. You are essentially building equity over the years, even if you don't have physical cash in hand. Eventually, your properties will appreciate in value, and you will also be able to purchase many more properties through this method, thereby building your real estate investment portfolio. This approach works well for people who do not need quick cash or who have longer-term financial goals.

People with Limited Capital

If you are someone who is starting off with limited capital, you can definitely get involved in both house flipping and BRRRR. However, house flipping is a bit riskier, and in many cases, you will need a large amount of money available to purchase the property and renovate it quickly. While you can take out loans for this, you must handle your finances very well to ensure that you don't go into debt or overextend yourself.

With the BRRRR method, you can get involved with a lower amount of capital on hand. This is because you are refinancing your properties and pulling out a majority of your original investment so that you can reinvest it. Essentially, you are using the same money to continue investing without having to invest more than the original amount. Just bear in mind that whichever form of real estate investing you are trying to pursue, some capital will be needed to get started, and real estate investing is a type of investment that requires significantly more upfront than many other types of investing.

Passive vs. Active Investors

Some investors prefer to be more hands-on and active in their investments, while others favor a more passive approach. Neither is right nor wrong, but it is important to understand what you are getting into and what you can handle. In general, house flipping is a more hands-on type of investment. During the time you are renovating the property, you'll need to oversee the entire process to ensure that everything is going well. You are also responsible for managing the finances and the contractors. Additionally, you must get involved with marketing and selling the property.

Many people don't realize how much work this entails because they hope to simply give directions to the contractors and then only get involved at the end when it's time to sell. However, this is not realistic. If you do not have the time or the capacity to be hands-on with the property, then house flipping might not be the best choice for you.

The BRRRR method is hands-on at the beginning, but once everything has stabilized, it becomes a more passive form of income. Once you have your properties and have found tenants, you don't really have to do much because you become a landlord, and you only need to get involved if there is a problem. The only other time you will have to be very hands-on is when you purchase another property and need to renovate it in order to rent it out again. You are in control of how many properties you have, so if you do not have the capacity to renovate and reestablish a property, then you can simply manage the ones that you currently have, and they will still bring you an income, even if you're not doing much.

EVALUATING SUITABILITY BASED ON PERSONAL FACTORS

Every investor is different, and that means it is essential to evaluate how suitable an investment style is based on your personal factors. Many different elements come into play when considering an investment style, and asking the right questions will yield the best results. Remember that there are no right or wrong answers, but it is important to be completely honest with yourself so that you can identify which investment style will be best for you.

Time Frame Considerations

When it comes to the timeframe in which you can access your investment funds, each of these investment methods offers something different. BRRRR is more about creating long-term wealth, which means you don't always have immediate access to your funds, whereas house flipping provides much quicker returns. If you are trying to determine which option is best for you, consider asking yourself some of the following questions:

- How soon do I need to see results and financial returns from my investments?
- Am I looking for something that will provide a quick profit, or do I want to build something that will last for a long time?
- Can I commit to the hands-on renovation process for the next couple of months, or do I prefer something more steady over time?

Cash Flow vs. Lump Sum

With house flipping, you can expect to receive a lump sum of money once you sell your property for a profit. You will not receive any additional money from this investment after it has been sold. In contrast, with the BRRRR method, you can anticipate smaller returns on investment over a longer period because you will be earning rental income while renting out the property. Here are some questions you can ask yourself to determine whether you prefer long-term cash flow or a short-term lump sum:

- Do I need a one-time payout, or am I more comfortable receiving small amounts of money consistently each month?

- Would I be disciplined enough to manage my finances properly if I received a lump sum from a house flip?
- Is it better for me to have an automatic monthly income that can help supplement my day job or cover some of my regular expenses?

Tax Implications

Whenever we talk about money, one aspect that always needs to be considered is the tax implications. When you are considering house flipping, you must understand that the profits you earn will be taxed as ordinary income. However, with the BRRRR method, you benefit from aspects such as depreciation and other tax deductions. With rental properties, you receive tax deductions that arise from homeownership as well as deductions that are specific to rentals. Here are the questions to ask yourself:

- Am I fully aware of the tax implications that come with receiving a large profit from a house flip?
- Do I believe that there are benefits to tax rates, depreciation, mortgage interest, and other tax advantages associated with rentals?
- Do I fully understand property tax in my state and what the implications are for both of these investment methods?

Risk Assessment

Any kind of investment comes with a certain level of risk; however, some investments are riskier than others. Additionally, you must consider the types of risks you will incur with each method. For example, when it comes to house flipping, you need to account for the risks of market fluctuations as well as unexpected renovation surprises. Not everything is clear-cut with this type of investment, and while you might plan to sell your property for a specific amount, this may not reflect the reality of the situation when you put the house on the market. Sometimes, the housing market takes a dive, and properties are simply selling for much less than you might have predicted. The risk of unexpected renovation costs is another significant concern, and anyone who has renovated a property will tell you that there are far more surprises than you might anticipate. You only fully understand the extent of the damage or the renovation costs while you are in the thick of it.

There are also definite risks associated with renting out a property. For example, you must be aware that tenant management comes with its own challenges. You might encounter a difficult tenant who makes your life incredibly challenging or one who simply does not pay their rent on time. This has implications for your financial planning, and it can be quite difficult to evict someone, depending on the laws in your country or state. Another risk associated with the BRRRR method is refinancing risks. In some cases, the process is not as straightforward as applying for refinancing and then simply getting approved. Nothing is set in stone until you have signed all of the papers.

With all of these risks in mind, here are some questions that can help you assess which kinds you can tolerate and which ones are simply not worth it for you:

- Am I capable of handling risks such as a delayed permit, a burst pipe, or a property that cannot be sold quickly?
- Do I prefer the risks associated with tenant issues or refinancing, or the risks related to market timing and renovation?
- If things do not go according to plan, which would stress me out the most: sitting on a property that is not selling or

dealing with a rental property that is vacant for an extended period?

Personality Fit

Another important aspect to consider is your personality. Each one of us is unique, and that means we all have our own personalities, which come with particular strengths, weaknesses, and preferences. Some people are more tolerant of risk, while others are more patient, and we also have individuals who might be a bit more cautious. Here are some questions that you can ask yourself to understand how your personality fits into the type of investment strategy you are considering:

- Do I like the idea of managing a property, making quick decisions, and being hands-on, or do I prefer something more stable and a slow burn when it comes to my investments?
- Does the idea of dealing with tenants and managing a property excite me or drain me?
- Do I prefer a predictable income that might take longer to establish, or am I able to handle short-term stress for a bigger short-term payoff?

In this chapter, we covered the differences between house flipping and the BRRRR method in real estate investing. It is crucial to understand both before you commit to a property investment. Regardless of which investment method you choose, one of the biggest challenges that beginners face is limited funds. In the next chapter, we will dive into practical methods to begin real estate investing without having substantial capital at your fingertips.

HOW TO GET STARTED WITHOUT A LOT OF MONEY

According to a 2023 report by the National Association of Realtors, only 26% of home buyers paid cash for their homes, while 74% relied on financing options (2024).

FINANCING OPTIONS THAT DON'T REQUIRE HUGE SAVINGS

Financing is undoubtedly a significant consideration when it comes to real estate investing. Most people simply do not have the capital to invest in cash and will need to explore various financing options to make their real estate dreams come true. The very idea of financing a property can deter people from investing because it seems like a tedious and difficult process. However, this is not necessarily the case, as there are financing options that offer flexibility and are more beginner-friendly.

FHA Loan

One option could be a Federal Housing Administration (FHA) loan, which is a loan insured by the government. With this type of loan, you are required to provide a lower down payment than with other, more traditional loans from a financial service provider or a bank. It is also more accessible for beginners because you might not need as high a credit score to be approved for this type of loan. These loans were designed to help people in lower-income brackets purchase property.

Even though the requirements for an FHA loan are lower than those for other types of property loans, there are still some criteria that must be met to obtain one. For example, you will need to have a credit score of at least 580 to qualify. A down payment is also required for this loan, but it can be as low as 3.5% (Segal 2025). Compared to the much higher down payment percentages required for other loans, this is significantly more accessible for people who do not have substantial finances or cash on hand. If you have a credit score lower than 580, you can still access this loan, but it will require a higher down payment. As you can see, there is a lot of flexibility with an FHA loan, making it more accessible to many people.

There are also some basic qualifications you need to meet to be considered for this type of loan. Some of these requirements include having a Social Security number, legally residing in the US, being of legal age, having a qualifying credit score, providing proof of employment, and demonstrating sufficient income to handle the loan. As with any other loan process, there are no guarantees that you will receive the loan. You will need to apply and go through the process, and once you are approved, you will have access to the funds.

One important aspect of this type of loan is the fact that the property needs to be your principal residence. This means that you cannot use this loan to finance property that you do not live in. This does put some restrictions in terms of investment potential, as you won't be able to use this loan to purchase a property to flip or to purchase a property immediately to rent out.

However, a detached or semi-detached house, townhouse, condominium, or anything similar can be FHA approved, and you can rent out a part of your residence. Typically, this method is called house hacking, where you live within a part of the property and rent out another part of it. Essentially, you are using the rent that you are getting from part of your property to pay off your entire mortgage, so you are living in the property for free.

VA Loan

This is a type of loan that is available through the US Department of Veterans Affairs. It helps active service members and their spouses become homeowners. This type of loan can be used to either purchase a property or build, improve, and repair one. It can also be used to refinance an existing mortgage. This type of loan has significant benefits over other types of loans if you are a veteran. There is no down payment required, and sometimes there is no private mortgage insurance required. Even though this is a type of loan that sounds very appealing to most people, there are only a few people who will qualify for it based on their veteran status. If you are a veteran or the spouse of a veteran, then you can consider this as an avenue for you.

Hard Money Lenders

A hard money loan works very differently from other types of loans you obtain from a bank or financial service provider. This type of loan is issued by an individual or a private company to help someone purchase a property. A hard money loan is backed by the property rather than the creditworthiness of the person taking out the loan. When you take out a traditional loan, you must prove that you will be able to pay it back with interest; however, with a hard money loan, you are putting up the property as collateral. If you are unable to repay the loan, the lenders can take the property from you and sell it to recover their money.

Since a hard money loan is backed by collateral rather than your credit score or borrowing history, it is much easier to obtain this type of loan. However, it is important to be aware that with this type of loan, you will be paying significantly more interest. The interest rate is set by the person or entity loaning you the money and can range anywhere from 10% to 18%. This can be risky if you plan to pay off the loan over a long period. If you are taking out a loan to flip a house, this could be a good option because you will be repaying the loan relatively quickly, so the interest won't have as much of an effect.

Private Lenders

A private lender is an individual or a company that offers a loan outside of a traditional mortgage loan. The entity or individual will fund the loan from their own resources. Since it is private, the person or entity loaning you the money will set the terms and conditions, which can vary greatly depending on who you are obtaining the loan from.

Even though these types of loans are privately managed, there are still some criteria that you need to meet in order to access them. Just bear in mind that this is definitely not set in stone, and you will have to talk with the lender to properly define their requirements. Typically, a down payment of around 20% or more is expected, as well as having the property professionally appraised for its value. You will also need a good credit score, which should be above 620, along with proof of income to demonstrate to the lender that you have the necessary funds to repay the loan (Martin 2025).

ALTERNATIVE ENTRY POINTS THAT DON'T REQUIRE BUYING RIGHT AWAY

In some cases, you might not want to purchase a property outright. There are some excellent options to still be able to have a property and make money from it without following the traditional methods.

House Hacking

House hacking is becoming increasingly popular for those looking to invest in real estate. We have already briefly mentioned what it is, but let's do a quick recap. House hacking is when you generate income from your home and then use that income to pay off your mortgage, allowing you to stay in the property for free. This can be done by dividing your property and living in one section while renting out the other for income. It is typically easier to house hack if you purchase a multifamily property, as it is simpler to divide it into different sections.

There are other ways to house hack without having a multifamily home; you just have to be a little more creative. For example, you could find a roommate to share your space with. You could also rent out your garage, yard space, or extra room as storage for people to keep their belongings. If you live in a densely populated area where parking is hard to come by, you could rent out a parking space. All of these options are great for house hacking, and you can even implement more than one, depending on the size and layout of your property.

Partnership

Another avenue you could explore is a real estate partnership. This is where you combine the strengths of two people to split the work and make things easier for both parties. In a partnership, there is typically a financial component as well as a time and effort component. One person might have the funds, while the other might have the expertise, time, and resources to manage the property and handle all of the real estate affairs. You can think of this as an active participant and a passive participant. These two different strengths, when combined, can lead to a lucrative investment opportunity for everyone involved.

When entering into a partnership with someone else, it is crucial to hash out all the details and draw up a contract so that everyone knows their responsibilities. Doing this at the beginning means that nobody will overstep their boundaries, which will cause much less friction down the line.

You could have a real estate limited partnership or a general partnership that falls under this category. In a real estate limited partnership, there is a general partner and a limited partner. The limited partner is the one who funds the investment, while the general partner takes care of the day-to-day operations regarding the investment. If you enter into a general partnership, it means that there is more than one person who will be a general owner and will be responsible for the day-to-day management and decisions regarding the investment. In this case, each partner will have equal rights and responsibilities in decision-making and all other matters concerning the property.

Wholesaling

Real estate wholesaling is an interesting approach to real estate investment. With this strategy, you purchase a property and then almost immediately sell it for a profit. You won't need to make any significant improvements or changes to the property; essentially, you are just acting as the middleman. For the strategy to work, you will need to be on the lookout for great deals when properties go on sale. You are looking to purchase a property that is sold below its market value so that you can make a profit when you resell it.

The turnaround time for property wholesaling should be quite quick to limit risks and enable you to receive your profit as soon as possible. This is typically done with distressed properties and individuals who are looking to sell their properties quickly. Once you find a property, you'll need to contact the seller and discuss how a wholesale real estate transaction works. You will then need to obtain a property contract, which must include the right to assign the contract to another party. You are not purchasing the property; rather, you are the person who will find someone to buy it. You will need to agree on how much the seller wants to make from the property so that you can keep the remainder as your profit.

Once all of this is in place, you will need to find a cash buyer. This is important because the seller will want the money as quickly as possible, and you will want your profit as well. Once everything is finalized, all you need to do is reassign the contract to the buyer and close the deal.

REAL EXAMPLES OF LOW-BUDGET DEALS

Jackson is someone who has a lot of experience in real estate and wants to use a hard money loan to help him make another real estate investment. As he was doing his research, he came across a distressed property that was in a really good neighborhood. He could see the potential in this property; all it needed was a little bit of love and some hard work. He knew that if he didn't make a move on this property, it was likely to be sold quite quickly, given that it was cheap and in a good area. He decided to take out a hard money loan since this was going to be the easiest and fastest option for him to obtain financing for the property.

Once he had access to the funds, he purchased the property, and it was time to get to work. He started renovating and updating the property to make it more modern and usable. Since it was an older property, it was very sturdy and well-made, so there weren't any huge structural changes that he had to make. He made sure to choose renovations that would provide a maximum return on his investment. He also ensured that he selected contractors he trusted and who were reputable in the real estate market. He didn't have the time or the money to waste on redoing something due to a botched job by an unreliable contractor.

The entire renovation process took about three months, and at this point, it was time to put the property on the market. Since the quality of work was high and the property looked great in a good area, it sold pretty quickly and at the price he was aiming for. He made a great return on investment through the profit he gained from the property. He was also able to pay off his hard money loan very quickly, so the high interest rate did not impact him significantly. This built his confidence in house flipping and real estate investing, so he continued doing it and made sure to conduct thorough research to make the process smoother and maximize his profit.

SIMPLE FIRST STEPS

Working toward your first real estate deal is an incredibly exciting process, but there are also steps you need to take to ensure that you are doing it properly. Let's take a look at these.

Check Your Credit Score

The first thing you'll need to do is check your credit score. Having a good credit score will significantly open up your options for obtaining a loan and financing your real estate investment. They say knowledge is power, so knowing your credit score is essential. This will help you determine whether you need to work on improving your score, and then you can create a plan to do this effectively over the next few months and years.

It is relatively easy to check your credit score. All you need to do is enter your information on your credit bureau's website, and it should pull up your credit information. You should actually check your credit score fairly often to ensure that there aren't any errors in your credit report and to confirm that you are moving in a positive direction.

Research Local Loan Programs

Every state has different loan programs, so it is important to understand which ones will be available to you before you even begin trying to finance a property. Simply conducting some internet research will help you discover what programs are available and what you need to do to qualify for them. If you don't qualify for a loan right now, you can create a plan to build yourself up to the point where you do qualify for one.

Make a List of Local Investor Meetups or Groups

Sharing ideas and knowledge with other investors is crucial. This is why getting together with other real estate investors is so important. You will gain insights and knowledge that you can't obtain anywhere else, plus other investors will be able to provide you with accurate advice based on their real experiences. They might also be able to assist you on your real estate journey, so making these connections is highly important.

You can look at social media or conduct an internet search to find your local investor meetups and groups. It might seem daunting to try joining one of these associations, but you'll find that people are much more helpful and friendly than you might think. Building your network is one of the most important things anyone can do in their professional life. We all need a helping hand sometimes, and having people who are in the same field as you is a great way to receive the right assistance and advice.

Talking to a Local Real Estate Agent or Mortgage Broker

When you are dealing with real estate, you will need to contact a real estate agent or a mortgage broker at some point. Doing this as early as possible is a great idea. Real estate agents possess extensive knowledge of the local real estate market, and they can help you understand the market you are trying to enter and what you need to do to be successful. They can offer guidance and tips on how to search for the right property, and they can assist you throughout the entire real estate process. A mortgage broker is an expert in the mortgage process, and they can help you understand what you need to do to qualify for a mortgage with a favorable interest rate. Building relationships with these types of professionals will aid you in your real estate investment journey and ensure that you are not scrambling to find these experts when you are ready to start investing or buying.

Investing can often seem very complicated and expensive, but there are many low-barrier ways to begin investing. Whether it's choosing nontraditional financing options or using an entry strategy like house hacking, you can definitely enter the real estate market with confidence as a beginner. Your first step does not have to be significant; it just needs to be intentional.

Hopefully, you now have the confidence to embark on your real estate journey. In the next chapter, we will shift gears so that you can learn how to find good deals and evaluate potential properties, setting yourself up for success. It is possible to start your real estate journey without a large down payment or the perfect financial situation. However, you do need to know how to identify the right property, and that will be our focus in the next chapter. The goal is to find undervalued properties, which will work for both house flipping and the BRRRR method.

PART II

TAKE ACTION AND MAKE SMART MOVES

3

FINDING THE RIGHT PROPERTIES

I n 2024, approximately 10% of real estate transactions were off-market deals, highlighting the growing importance of alternative sourcing methods in a competitive market (Dodge 2025).

EXPLORING PROPERTY SOURCING METHODS

Having a solid plan to secure financing for your real estate investment is the first step. Now that that's out of the way, we can focus on how to find potential investment properties. Just because you can afford a property or it looks good on the outside, doesn't mean it will make a great investment. Therefore, it is important to understand what you are doing when searching for a real estate investment property.

Multiple Listing Service (MLS)

A multiple listing service is a database that a real estate agent creates based on the information they have for a particular area. This is a handy tool for real estate agents because it allows other agents to see the MLS and connect buyers to various listings. Someone looking to purchase a property can also consult an MLS to find information about properties that are on the market and then make comparisons. Typically, this kind of database is electronic and online, making it easily updated and accessible for everyone. You can contact your local real estate agent and ask for their MLS if you cannot easily find it online. You will need to partner with a real estate agent in the area to gain access to some of these databases.

There is a wealth of information available on an MLS that can help you make better decisions when searching for a potential property. The information in each database will depend on the real estate agent who set it up. However, some information you can expect to see includes sales data, the structural components of the property, the interior features, and any special attributes.

Off-Market Deals

Most properties that are up for sale can be found on a multiple listing service, but there are also other ways to find a property. These are known as off-market homes, and they might provide you with the opportunity to access a better deal through a private avenue. They are more exclusive than the properties listed on an MLS, and only a single real estate agent will handle the buying and selling of them.

The reason a real estate agent might want to keep this information to themselves is that it results in less competition in the real estate market. It is also better for flexible negotiation since buyers and sellers can speak directly with one another to come up with a deal that works best for everyone. Additionally, there won't be the added pressure of traditional real estate sales timelines or the stress of having multiple people making offers on the property at the same time.

Finding an off-market listing can be a bit more difficult. Your best bet is to contact your local real estate agent and ask them directly if they have any off-market homes currently available. Another avenue to explore is online property websites. You might need to survey quite a few properties to find what you're looking for. However, if there are filters, see if you can filter by unlisted or for-sale-by-owner options.

Another important tool when looking for off-market properties is networking and approaching homeowners directly. If you have a network, see if you can put out feelers to indicate that you are interested in purchasing an off-market property, and then simply wait to see who responds. Your network is a very powerful tool because you never know who can assist you in your real estate investment journey. Building a network is something you will continuously do as you meet more people. This will be an ongoing part of your real estate journey, so working on your networking skills is key.

APPLYING INVESTMENT RULES

There are a few very helpful investment rules that you can use when investing in real estate. The rules you will be using will also depend on the type of real estate investment you are pursuing and what you plan to do with your property.

70% Rule for Flipping

The 70% rule is a great guideline for flipping a house. Essentially, when you take on a house-flipping project, the goal is to purchase your property for as low a price as possible so that you can reap a much larger profit when you sell. If you spend too much money on buying the house and on renovations, you will struggle to achieve any reasonable profit when you sell the house. This is why it is important to know what the home's sale price will be before you start making any purchases. This is where the 70% rule comes in to help you.

With the 70% rule, you should not pay more than 70% of your property's after-repair value, subtracting the cost of the repairs and renovations you will be making to the property. The after-repair value is simply the amount that the property could possibly sell for after you have fixed it up. To use this rule, you will need to estimate how much you think the property will sell for, multiply that by 70%, and then subtract your estimated renovation costs.

From here, you will arrive at the maximum amount you can pay for a property while still achieving a good profit. Just remember that this rule is simply a guideline to help you determine how much a property is worth or how much you should be paying for it. It is not a hard and fast rule that you must abide by. Other factors may come into play that could sway your decision or change the amount you need to pay for a property.

Also, remember that this method relies on many estimations, which means there are limitations to its accuracy. This is why it is crucial to spend some time researching the market and ensuring that you understand its ups and downs. This will also provide you with an indicator of what you can expect from the market and help you make better decisions going forward.

1% Rule for Rentals

The 1% rule is a useful guideline that you can apply with the BRRRR method or any other real estate investing strategy where you plan to rent out a property. With this rule, you simply multiply the purchase price of the property, including any necessary repairs, by 1%. The resulting figure will represent the amount of monthly rent you can set as your baseline when renting out the property. Although this is not a hard and fast rule, it provides a good estimate of your potential monthly cash flow when renting out your property.

It offers a starting point, but it is advisable to consider other factors, such as the general market rate in your area. You may have acquired a property at a bargain price and are paying a very low amount for a property in a desirable location. In this case, you might be able to charge more for rent than what the 1% rule suggests. You would use the 1% rule as your baseline and then take additional factors into account to maximize your rental profit.

UTILIZING ANALYTICAL TOOLS

These days, there are numerous tools at your disposal. You can leverage these to your advantage and simplify your real estate journey.

After-Repair Value (ARV) Calculators

The formula to calculate the after-repair value is straightforward: After-Repair Value = Purchase Price + Renovation Cost. However, you do not need to do the math yourself, as there are online calculators that perform all the calculations for you. These tools are user-friendly and accurate because they also consider other factors, such as the location of your property. One of these calculators can be found here: https://tools.reikit.com/comps/.

Return on Investment (ROI) Calculators

The goal of an investment is to make you money, so knowing the return on investment (ROI) is vital. This knowledge will help you predict how much you will gain from your investment. You can use this information to decide whether this is a good investment. The ROI is expressed as a percentage; therefore, the higher the percentage, the better the investment. There are two methods that can be used to calculate ROI: the cost method and the out-of-pocket method.

The basic formula for calculating ROI is as follows:

ROI = (Investment Gain – Investment Cost) / Investment Cost

Let's discuss the cost method first. With this method, you take into consideration the total cost of the investment. This encompasses the price you paid to buy the property and the cost of any renovations or improvements made. For example, if you bought a property for $100,000, spent $20,000 fixing it up, and then sold it for $160,000, you would calculate it as follows:

(160,000 – 120,000) / 120,000 = 33%

The out-of-pocket method is based on your invested money. It factors in the use of borrowed or leveraged money, so you would typically see a higher number when calculating the ROI. Let's use similar numbers as above. The purchase price of the property is $100,000, with a down payment of $30,000. The renovations cost you $20,000, which makes your out-of-pocket expenses $50,000. You sold the property for $160,000. Now, use these numbers to calculate ROI:

(160,000 – 120,000) / 50,000 = 80%

A good ROI calculator can be found here: https://www.calculator.net/roi-calculator.html.

Deal Analysis Software

There is a lot that goes into analyzing a deal, but you do not have to do everything yourself because there are platforms that do most of it for you. The ones I recommended you check out are:

- DealCheck: https://dealcheck.io/
- DealMachine: https://www.dealmachine.com/
- PropStream: https://www.propstream.com/
- Mashvisor: https://www.mashvisor.com/

SELECTING THE RIGHT MARKET AND NEIGHBORHOOD

It is crucial to choose the right neighborhood when investing in real estate. This decision can make or break your investment, so it is essential to conduct thorough research when selecting the neighborhood. A real estate market analysis is also known as a comparative market analysis. This is where you analyze the current market values of properties and compare them to the property you are considering buying or selling. This is one of the best and easiest ways to conduct a real estate market analysis.

When performing this type of comparative market analysis, the goal is to help you decide whether or not you should invest in a specific area. This is especially helpful if you are wondering about purchasing a property in two or three different cities. You can compare and determine which option is better. This type of market analysis also helps you identify elements that could potentially hinder the success of your investment in certain areas. Additionally, you will gain insight into the demographics of the area, allowing you to fully understand the future potential of the neighborhood. All of these factors are essential for understanding your potential investment. Let's delve into more detail about the steps you will need to follow to conduct a market analysis.

Step 1: Be Informed About the Market

The first step is always to be informed about the market. You need to understand the market you are working with in order to make the best decisions regarding it. In this initial step, you should look at things from a global or broad perspective without delving deeply into the specifics or details. This broad perspective is necessary to form the foundation of your analysis and ensure that you understand the situation from a larger viewpoint.

The real estate market is always evolving and changing, so it's important to stay on top of what is happening, as well as observe the trends. Take a look at what the real estate market looks like now and how it is performing. You can gain valuable insights into what the market might look like by examining economic indicators; if the economy is doing well, it will likely be reflected in the real estate market as well.

It is also a good idea to analyze your competitors to see what they are offering or doing so that you can gain a better understanding for yourself. If they are being more aggressive with their investment strategies, try to understand why this is the case, and then see if you can apply a similar strategy to your investments. It is not advisable to simply copy someone else's investment strategy or analysis of the market, so make sure that you conduct your own research and support what you observe with your competitors using your knowledge and expertise.

Step 2: Know the Customers in the Market

Knowing your customers is vital when you are trying to understand a market or when you are investing in real estate in general. This can also be referred to as understanding the current demand in the market. Who is looking for what kind of property? How many people are searching for property? What is attracting potential customers to certain properties? These are all great questions to start asking yourself so that you can fully understand the potential customers in the market.

A good starting point is to ask yourself how many customers are currently in the real estate market and how this is changing over time. A market analysis is not something you will conduct at one static point; rather, it is something you will continuously perform to track changes to understand how things are evolving. See if you can identify whether the demand is increasing, decreasing, or remaining the same. You will also need to know who your real estate customers are and where they are located. Examine their consumption rates and behaviors. It might also be beneficial to understand what the budget of your customers is, as well as the common factors that tend to trigger a purchase.

Step 3: Study in Detail What Your Competitors Already Offer

You might not be too excited about having many competitors, but you can use your competition to your advantage. When you have direct competition, it means that you and a few others are all competing for the same customers or potential investment opportunities. This indicates that your competitors have been researching matters pertaining to you and your investments as well. Consequently, you can obtain vital information by studying their behavior and gaining a deeper understanding of it.

The first thing you will need to do is figure out who your competitors in the market are. They could be individual investors or even larger companies. Try to determine their investment strategies and whether or not they have been successful over the long term. Examine their trends as well as any public financial data you can find. All of this will help you understand your competitors more deeply, and it will also assist you in grasping the market in which they operate. If someone else has made a mistake that did not work out, you can learn from their errors rather than repeating the same ones yourself. This will help you achieve greater success in a shorter period of time, so it is definitely something you should not overlook.

Step 4: Analyze the Factors That May Influence the Market

There are many factors that could potentially influence the market that may not be directly related to actual real estate. For example, there may have been technological developments, or new laws and regulations might have been enacted. There may also be a new real estate trend that emerges, making certain properties more attractive than others.

Step 5: Collect Data to Determine If the Project Is Viable and Secure

Data collection is an underrated but very important part of real estate market research. When you collect data, you are essentially gathering information that will assist you in determining whether a project is a good investment or if it is something you need to move on from. Some of the data you will need to collect includes demographic and socioeconomic information. This is important because it will help you understand the demand for the property and what is happening in the area. For example, if there is an area experiencing a large influx of younger families, this indicates that it is an affordable area, and the demand for housing will likely increase over the next few years.

You can use various tools to help you collect and analyze the data for the property or area in which you are looking to invest. Some of the most helpful tools include property management software, such as a real estate CRM system, which helps you manage your real estate portfolio. You can also examine heat maps, which will show you where there is high demand for properties and where there is potential for growth. You might even want to conduct property surveys in the area to gain a more hands-on understanding of what is happening locally.

Evaluate a Neighborhood Before Investing

When it comes to investing in property, it can be more important to invest in a good area than to focus solely on a specific property. When you consider purchasing a property, you will likely choose an area first and then look for properties within that area to see if anything meets your needs and standards. Typically, it does not work the other way around, where you would search for a specific property and then evaluate the area to see if it suits your requirements. A specific neighborhood or area will have benefits and amenities that align with the lifestyles of certain individuals, which is why selecting the right neighborhood is so crucial for investors.

Regardless of who your target customer or tenant is, it is important to consider the amenities that are close to your potential property investment. The more amenities that are nearby, the better your chances of attracting the right kinds of tenants. It is true that different demographics will desire different amenities. For example, a young single person who is just starting out in their career might want to be closer to city life, with social meetup spots like restaurants and bars nearby, whereas families are looking for proximity to good schools, parks, and family-friendly facilities. In general, you would like the neighborhood you are investing in to have good schools, restaurants, shops, gyms, medical facilities, and recreational activities close by.

Another key indicator of a good area is its proximity to employment. Many people choose to live close to where they work, so if there are many job opportunities in an area, it will be attractive to a lot more people. This doesn't necessarily mean that it has to be in the economic hub, but being near an area with more job availability is advantageous. You should also consider factors like crime rates, as everyone would prefer to live in a place with a lower crime rate.

If you want to get a good idea of what is happening in a specific neighborhood or area, it is advisable to get in your car and drive around or walk through the neighborhood. You will see what is actually going on, apart from what you can research. If you notice a lot of rundown properties where it appears that the residents do not take pride in their homes, this is not a good sign. It is also a red flag if you see many signs indicating "for rent" or "for sale." You don't want a large number of vacant properties in an area, as this indicates that people do not want to live there and that more people are moving out than moving in. The only exception would be a neighborhood or area with a lot of new development and new builds, as this will naturally have more properties for sale or rent.

Even though it can seem like a tedious job, doing your research on the neighborhood and the properties you want to invest in is a key part of the real estate investment journey. It is going to save you a lot of time, money, and resources in the long run, and you'll be thankful that you spent a little extra effort doing the groundwork before putting down your money for an investment. The great thing is that there are many tools available that can really help you ensure you have the best chance at a successful investment, so it is a good idea to use these to your advantage. The goal is to be able to make the most informed decisions you can as you embark on your real estate investment journey.

Now that you can identify promising properties, your next step is to understand how to effectively rehabilitate a property to maximize its value and your potential returns. In the next chapter, we will dive into the renovation process so that you can understand key elements such as budgeting, planning, and executing successful property rehabilitation.

REHAB WITHOUT REGRET

I n 2024, Americans spent an estimated $603 billion on home remodeling, with 46% of home buyers being less willing to compromise on the condition of the home when purchasing (National Association of Realtors 2025). This highlights the importance of well-executed renovations in the real estate market.

THE REHAB PROCESS

There is a lot that goes into the rehab process when it comes to real estate. Knowing the full extent of what is expected is fundamental to ensuring your success. Let's discuss some of the things you will need to consider as you embark on this journey.

The first thing you need to do is plan and work out your design for your property. Many people like to skip this step because it seems like a waste of time, and they believe it will take too long. If you are the type of person who just likes to dive into something, then the planning and preparation phase is probably the part you will dislike the most. However, it is one of the most important things you can do to ensure a smooth process from start to finish.

Think about building a house from scratch; you will want to make sure that the foundation is set and solid before you start with anything else. If you do not have a solid and secure foundation, as you continue building your house, there is a risk that the foundation will give way, ruining all the hard work you have put in throughout the rest of the process. Then, you will need to break down everything you have done and start from the bottom again. I'm sure this is not something you want to do, which is why it is important to recognize that planning and preparation are the foundation of everything else that comes afterward.

If you are undertaking a larger renovation, you will also need to consider the time and resources required for the demolition. You might want to remove a certain part of the property to create space for something else, or it may simply be an eyesore that you wish to eliminate. Following that, the rebuilding phase will commence, during which you will begin to see tangible progress toward making the space look the way you envision. In some cases, the rebuilding phase may not take too long; however, if you are making significant changes to the property, you should plan for it to be quite resource-intensive and time-consuming. Additionally, you will need to consider the installation of essential systems such as plumbing, HVAC, electrical, and mechanical components. All of this is crucial to ensure that your property and home function at their best and meet all safety standards.

Once you have the structure and these important elements in place, you can move on to your walls and flooring. It may be the case that you do not need to break down or build up much, so you would only need to redo the flooring or certain walls. Other tasks you might need to undertake include adding cabinets, appliances, and final touches. This is definitely the more enjoyable part of the process, as you can see your vision coming to life; however, it requires careful planning and time to get it right. Along the way, you may discover that some of your initial plans do not work out as expected, necessitating adjustments. This is a very normal part of the process, and it is something you should anticipate. Let's discuss in more depth the steps you will take as you navigate the rehabilitation process.

Step 1: Make a Plan

As mentioned above, it is crucial to start your process by making a solid plan. This is where you establish your priorities so you know exactly what you will be working on first and how you will proceed through the process. It also helps you stay on track and ensures that you do not get caught up in details that are not important.

Step 2: Set a Budget

Part of the planning process is budgeting, which is essential. It is easy to go off course and spend significantly more money than you have available. When you budget, you can allocate your funds to the most important items and ensure that you will not run out at crucial moments. When budgeting, make sure to keep about 10% to 20% of the total amount for unforeseen circumstances and expenses. As much as planning is essential, unexpected bumps in the road can arise, and it is important to have the finances to help you navigate through them.

Step 3: Hire a Contractor

Once you have set your budget, it is time to hire your contractors. If you have been through the renovation process before, you probably have one or two contractors with whom you are comfortable. If not, then it is time to start interviewing. Take your time with this, as you will be entering into a contract with this person and including them in a significant portion of the renovation process. Ensure that they have the necessary skills, certifications, and experience to help you achieve your goals. Do not choose the cheapest or most convenient option in this case.

Step 4: Talk to Your Insurance Company

You will need to ensure that you have the necessary insurance coverage, so call your insurance company before and after the renovation process is completed. Remember that when you renovate a property, it increases in value; therefore, the amount for which you were insured at the beginning of the process may not be sufficient afterward.

Step 5: Secure Permits and Order Materials

Before you start breaking ground on your renovation, it is important to ensure that you have all of the necessary permits and materials. Every county and state has different requirements regarding permits and what they allow in general. Understanding the permits you will need will help you ensure a smooth process and avoid incurring any unnecessary fines. At this stage, you should also begin securing your materials for the remainder of the building process.

Step 6: Start Demolition

Once all of this is done, you can start the demolition of the property. This is not always necessary, and it really depends on the size of your project. However, if you are undertaking significant renovations, then demolition is an important step. Even something as simple as relocating a wall requires some demolition, so keep this in mind.

Step 7: The Installs

Once the demolition is complete, you can begin rebuilding and installing the necessary and important elements. For example, you will need to finish the patching, drywall, sanding, painting, flooring, appliances, and cabinetry.

Step 8: Add the Finishing Touches

Once all that is done, it is time for you to add the finishing touches to your property. You'll want to incorporate some fixtures and hardware that will make things look appealing. This will include lighting, door handles, a backsplash, and even sealing the floor so that it looks crisp and new. You can also add other design elements, but it depends on what you are doing with the property. If you are renting out the property and choosing to do so fully furnished, then you'll need to furnish the property and ensure that it attracts the type of tenant you want. If you are planning to sell the property, then you do not need to worry about furniture or making things look pretty.

ESTIMATING COSTS AND AVOIDING SURPRISES

It can be very easy to let the cost of revamping your property skyrocket without proper planning. Expenses can quickly add up, and because you are likely to spend smaller amounts of money on many different items, it might be difficult to track. Being able to estimate your costs effectively will help you avoid any surprises down the line and ensure that you have enough money for the most important aspects of your renovation journey.

Step 1: Pick Your Projects

When you purchase a property with potential, you might have a long list of different things you want to do to increase its value. However, not all of these things will be realistic based on your timeline or budget. This is why it is so important to select the projects you want to tackle during your renovation. Since you are renovating to increase the potential profit of your property, it is best to write down a list of all the things you want to do and then prioritize them based on what would add the most value. Adding an extra bedroom or bathroom might be more beneficial than retiling the kitchen. Even though it might be nice to install new floors in the kitchen and it would increase the value, adding an extra room will be much more valuable and yield more money in the long run. It's all about planning and being smart about where you invest your money so that you can achieve the best returns while spending the least.

Step 2: Research the Costs

You will need to understand the costs associated with each of your renovation projects. There are many hidden costs that are not immediately obvious, which means that conducting thorough research will help you uncover these hidden expenses, allowing you to obtain an accurate representation of how much you will be spending. For something like retiling a floor, you will need to spend money on tiles, but that is not the only expense. You will also need cement or adhesive to adhere the tiles to the floor, as well as grout. Additionally, you might require a sealant, tools to complete the tiling job, and equipment to remove the previous flooring.

You will also need to consider the contractors or professionals you will hire to complete this job. You can consult a contractor with a specific skill set for the project you wish to undertake and ask them for an estimate of how much everything will cost, including labor. Be sure to add a little extra as a buffer in case unexpected costs arise.

Step 3: Keep a List of All Your Cost Estimates

Keeping a list will help you track all of the cost estimates you made during the planning stage. You can update this list, but it is also important to do your best to adhere to it throughout the process. This list should organize your total budget into different categories, so you know how much is allocated to each area. You can break this down into specific percentages, with the highest percentage going toward the most expensive or most important items.

Step 4: Set Your Savings Goal

Once you have estimated the costs of everything you want to do, it's time to start saving and budgeting. This is something you need to do in advance so that you have enough time to save for all the renovations you want to undertake. Depending on the type of project you are going to pursue, whether it's flipping a house or following the BRRRR framework, you might need a larger amount of money. You will be able to leverage some of the expenses through a loan so that you aren't paying the majority of the expenses out of pocket or in cash. However, it is a good idea to have some physical funds available for renovating the property. Once you know your total savings goal, you can break it down into smaller amounts to start working toward that goal.

Step 5: Collect Bids from Contractors

Now is the time to interview and collect bids from contractors. Remember what we discussed earlier: the cheapest, most convenient option might not be the best one. This is why it is so important to do your research and conduct interviews with each of your contractors. If you can obtain reviews or referrals from other people you trust who have used these contractors, that is even better, as it provides firsthand experience of how good or bad they are. You can also conduct some online research to find out if there are any online reviews, which will help you better understand your potential contractors.

Step 6: Schedule Your Renovation

Once all of this is done, your planning is almost complete, and it's time to schedule your renovation. This includes ensuring that all elements are aligned so you can start on a specific day. You will want to make sure that you have all the appropriate materials and contractors available around the same time to avoid losing precious hours due to missing materials or unavailable contractors. It helps to schedule a bit in advance to ensure that everything goes according to plan and that you have everything you need. This also gives you some time to prepare for the process ahead, which might be quite a significant task to undertake.

HIGH-ROI UPGRADES AND DIY TIPS

ROI stands for return on investment, and it refers to the amount of profit you will make after completing your investment in relation to how much money you spent. Every investor seeks to achieve a higher ROI, which means spending less money to generate more profit. Certain renovations and DIY projects yield a much higher ROI, and those are the areas you can focus on to ensure you maximize your profit. Let's discuss a few of these options, and then you can decide which ones will be best for you.

One upgrade that can bring a higher ROI is a garage door replacement. In many cases, the garage door is one of the first things people see when they enter a property. Having a modern, clean, and aesthetically pleasing garage door will significantly enhance curb appeal. Additionally, it is not very expensive, so you could potentially double your ROI with just this improvement. Continuing with the theme of curb appeal, you can replace your entry door to create a more expensive and modern look. This is something that people will notice from the outside, and they will expect something amazing on the inside as well. Plus, there is nothing better than walking through a beautifully designed doorway.

One of the most frequently used rooms in a house is the kitchen, which truly attracts potential buyers. Updating and replacing a few key elements in the kitchen can significantly increase a property's perceived value. These updates include updating countertops, replacing hardware, installing new flooring, repainting walls, and improving lighting. You can also make a few adjustments by rearranging certain amenities to enhance user-friendliness.

Everyone loves an outdoor space for enjoyment and entertaining, which is why a deck could be a great addition to your property. An outdoor deck is one of the features that truly attracts buyers to a home. The most popular types of decks are wood and composite, so you will need to choose which one best suits your needs and budget. Composite decks are more expensive, but they offer a better return on investment and are highly durable.

Another room that can significantly enhance resale value is the bathroom. There is nothing better than a modern and relaxing bathroom. When bathrooms are outdated and old-looking, they do not feel as welcoming or inviting, which can deter many potential buyers or renters from purchasing or renting a property. Adding new fixtures, tiles, lighting, and decor can greatly help modernize and improve a bathroom.

A few other aspects to consider are window replacements. This is especially relevant if the house is quite old and the windowpanes appear incredibly outdated. You can also look into replacing the floors or the roof if these elements are not up to standard or do not look as nice as they could. This depends on how much money you have to spend on renovations and should be considered last, after you have evaluated the other areas we have already discussed.

Now, remember that some tasks can definitely be done by yourself, while others require professional assistance. While it might be tempting to do everything yourself to cut costs, this can lead to bigger issues down the line. Therefore, make sure that you only undertake DIY projects that are suitable. For example, you can certainly repaint walls, replace small fixtures, change the lighting, install simple tiles, install kitchen cabinets or doors, update knobs and door handles, clean the gutters, power wash the outdoor area, and tidy up the outdoor landscape. Tasks that you should definitely hire a professional for include electrical work, plumbing, major renovations, siding, roof repairs, and structural or foundational repairs.

RECOGNIZING AND AVOIDING RED FLAGS

On this journey, there are some red flags that you should do your best to avoid in order to prevent any wasted money down the line. When looking for a potential property in which you will be investing, this is when you need to be extra alert. Certain issues can cost you significantly more money and simply won't be worth renovating, and these are the things you should avoid.

The number one item on the list is foundation problems. If a house has foundation issues, it means that you will essentially have to redo the entire house, as you will need to dismantle the existing structure before fixing the foundation. This is definitely not worth it and will require a lot of work and money. You should also look out for signs of wear and tear and an outdated design in the property. Some homes have been around for a very long time, and the general wear and tear of the structure of the property may not be what it should be. It might take considerable work and renovations to ensure that the house is modern and fully functional before you can sell or rent it out.

Another aspect to consider is safety concerns or limited function-ality with certain features of the property. You want to make sure that the property is 100% safe, and you also want to ensure that it is user-friendly. If the current layout or design of the property doesn't align with how modern people live, then it's really not going to be worth it. For example, I have seen properties where the bathrooms are outside of the main building, which seems like a nightmare for anyone living in that home on a day-to-day basis.

Significant issues like water damage, pest problems, and general environmental concerns are also things you will need to avoid if you are trying to achieve a higher ROI. The goal is to spend the least amount of money while obtaining the most returns, so when these major issues arise, it will require a lot of time, energy, and resources to resolve, making it potentially not the best choice for an investment.

Spotting Unreliable Contractors

You will need a reliable contractor throughout the process, so it's important to spot any potential red flags early on to avoid engaging further with a bad contractor. There are a few things you can consider red flags when getting a quote or thinking about moving forward with a specific contractor. One thing to be wary of is if the contractor is asking for a large down payment or if the contract is very vague. It is easy to be taken advantage of in both of these cases, so it's important for you to read through the contract and ensure it is highly specific to the job and the tasks that need to be completed. Additionally, make sure that you do not have to pay an unnecessarily large down payment that is nonrefundable should the job not be done as needed.

Another red flag to consider is if the contractor has a lot of bad reviews or no reviews at all. You want a solid track record to ensure that this person will do what they say and is good at their job. If there are no reviews or no one for you to call for references, then this is definitely something you can consider a red flag, and you should move on from this potential contractor. An estimate or bid that is extremely low is also a red flag because it could indicate that this person does not know their worth, is just starting out, or is simply trying to make a quick buck without planning to do the job properly.

You can also learn a lot from a person's communication skills. If they are not communicating effectively, missing your messages, or simply going silent for long periods, then this is not someone you want to work with on a long project. You will also need to verify your potential contractors to ensure that they have the necessary licenses; if the information does not match up, then this person is probably shady and not someone you want to work with.

Other things that can be considered red flags include asking for upfront cash payments, appearing unprofessional, or even being under the influence of alcohol or other substances. All of these behaviors are simply unprofessional, and you don't want to work with someone who will bring negative energy to your project. You want someone professional and reliable.

At the end of the day, the planning phase is likely one of the most important phases of any renovation or real estate journey. It will be extremely helpful if everything is planned properly, as this ensures that things will go much more smoothly for you moving forward. It will also help you build a proper strategy and avoid potential mishaps and mistakes because you've already planned for or anticipated them before they occur. Even though it might seem tedious, it is definitely worth it to do your research and take your time with the planning process.

Now that you have a solid understanding of the renovation process, you are ready for the next step. This will involve diving into the BRRRR strategy. In the next chapter, we will fully explore how to leverage the buy, rehab, rent, refinance, repeat method to build a scalable and profitable real estate portfolio.

THE BRRRR PROCESS

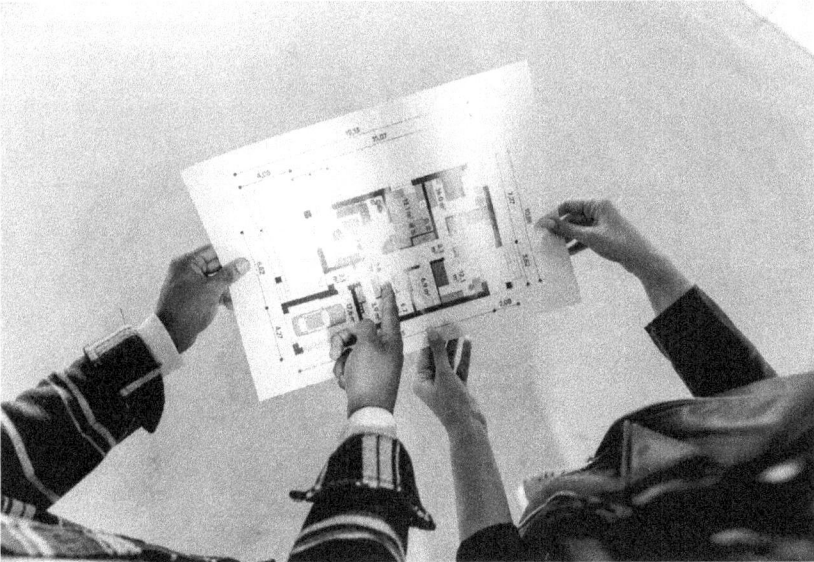

T he BRRRR method is a fantastic approach to entering real estate investing due to its structured nature. Many people have found success with it, but it's important to understand the process before diving in. When you fully comprehend the process and what goes into something like this, you can make better decisions, and you can navigate this type of real estate investment much more effectively. There are numerous individuals with fantastic success stories related to this method of real estate investing, and you can be one of them.

THE BRRRR STRATEGY: A CLOSER LOOK

There are five specific steps in the BRRRR method, and each letter represents something very important. In this section, we will discuss each of these steps and explore them in greater depth so that you fully understand each one.

Buy

The first step is to buy a property. This is what the "B" stands for in BRRRR. In this initial step, you need to ensure that you are purchasing the right property to maximize your investment. This step is not only the first but also the most important. If you buy the right property, it will make all the other steps much easier and ensure that you achieve a great ROI. The goal is to purchase a property as cheaply as possible, with as few issues as possible. You should be looking for a property that is below market value. Distressed or undervalued properties can offer significant rewards after the rehabilitation process.

During this phase, you will need to conduct market research to find the right property. It will take some time, and you are unlikely to find an ideal property within the first few days. Don't get disheartened; make sure to take your time so that you don't rush into something that could cost you later on. Once you have located your ideal property, it is time to start applying for a loan to purchase it. You will also need to obtain the appropriate licensing and registration required for the potential renovations you will be undertaking.

Rehab

The second step is the rehab step. This step focuses on a lot of what we discussed in the previous chapter. It's all about renovating and rehabilitating the property so that it is ready for your potential tenant. During this step, you will also ensure that you are selecting the right contractors to work on your project.

Rent

Once your property is ready, it is time to rent it out. The goal is to secure reliable tenants who will be able to pay you your weekly or monthly rental fee so that you can make a profit. It's not only about finding the right tenant but also about setting the right rental rate to ensure a consistent cash flow. There is a lot that goes into this, but conducting some market research and evaluating how much you want to charge based on what similar properties in the area are charging is a good start. Doing this at the beginning will help you get a better idea of what you can expect once your property is up for rent.

This step also includes marketing your property to get the word out and find the right tenant. The goal should be to have as many options as possible so that you can make the best choice. Marketing could involve strategies such as online ads, newspaper ads, word-of-mouth, or even posters and billboards. It all depends on your area and what will give you the most reach.

Once the word is out and people start applying to rent your property, you will need to conduct interviews and check references to ensure that you choose the right person. You should be very wary of anyone who applies without any references. Also, make sure you perform a credit check to ensure that the person renting can afford to pay the rent.

Refinance

Once you have your tenant, it is time for the fourth step, which is refinancing. With this step, you can pull out equity from the property to use for purchasing another property and repeating the process. This step requires a lot of accounting and ensuring that your finances are in order. Throughout this process, you must manage your property well and maintain it so that your tenants are happy. You will also need to communicate effectively with your tenants and ensure that you are meeting all of the lease agreements on your end.

Repeat

The final step is to repeat, which means that you will start again with the buying process and follow the steps once more. The goal of the BRRRR method is to grow your portfolio and maximize your profit. When you repeat the strategy, it means that you will manage multiple properties simultaneously. This does require some strategy, which may mean that you need to acquire software to assist you with property management. You might also consider hiring a property manager who will take care of the day-to-day operations of your properties while you focus on building your portfolio.

RISKS BEFORE INVESTING

As with any kind of investing, there are definitely risks associated with this method. It is important to understand these risks before proceeding so that you aren't going in blind. It will also help you to develop some contingency plans should one of these risks become a reality for you.

The first and probably the biggest risk is over-leveraging. There is great potential to make a lot of money through leveraging, which is why this method is so attractive; however, over-leveraging is something you need to watch for. Over-leveraging is essentially borrowing too much money and then being unable to pay it back. You might be tempted to stretch your borrowing capacity to secure the deal you want, but when you borrow too much money, you negatively impact your cash flow, making it difficult to repay the loan.

Another point regarding over-leveraging is that if the market experiences a downturn, your property value may decline. If you have a very small buffer between the money you've leveraged and what you possess, this could lead to significant problems. It could place you in a negative equity situation, which could complicate refinancing and obtaining loans. You want to ensure that your property can stand on its own two feet, even in the event of a market downturn. It is important not to rush into the next deal quickly after renting out one of your properties. You want to ensure that the properties you currently own are secure and can operate independently before you attempt to invest further.

Another risk is underestimating the rehabilitation costs of a property. This is something we have mentioned before, and it is incredibly common. The truth is that you never truly know how much the rehabilitation will cost until you are in the thick of it. This is why it is important to do your best to estimate, but also to have a buffer amount so that if something unexpected arises, you have funds to cover it.

Along the same lines, the risk of overestimating the after-repair value is very real. This occurs when you believe that you can rent or sell your property for much more than what is actually reflected in reality. This may happen because you didn't conduct your research properly, or the market has shifted since you made your estimates. This is why it is so important to stay up-to-date with your local real estate news and to be more conservative with your estimates.

Since the BRRRR method is all about renting and finding tenants, there is a risk of getting a bad tenant who could cause more issues than benefits for you. For example, a tenant could cause property damage, lead to legal disputes, or fail to pay their rent, and all of this will be your responsibility. Another risk associated with renting is that the market may not be in your favor. It could be difficult to find a tenant, which means you will have a higher vacancy rate, and every month your property remains vacant is money lost.

Another risk involves challenges with refinancing. You may find it difficult to secure favorable refinancing terms, which means you will not be getting a good deal on your loan, and it will cost you more than you expected. Even worse, you might not be able to obtain a loan or refinance your property at all. This is why it is so important to ensure that your credit score is good and that you have established relationships with lenders so that they trust you.

KEY CONSIDERATIONS DURING REFINANCING

When refinancing your property, your aim is to secure a lower interest rate or to completely change the repayment terms of your current mortgage. This helps you save on your monthly payments, allowing you to free up more finances for other purposes. In this case, you will have more money to invest in other properties and continue growing your real estate investment portfolio.

When you refinance your mortgage, you have the opportunity to lower the interest rate you currently have, which means that over the long term, you will be paying much less for the property. You might also be able to lower the monthly premium you need to pay and obtain a shorter loan term, which all adds up to additional savings. Refinancing also allows you to change your current mortgage product to something more beneficial or better suited to you at this moment. Sometimes, we might choose an option that seems like a good idea, but as time goes on, a better option becomes available for refinancing. One of the biggest benefits of refinancing is that you can cash out some of your equity and then secure a larger loan. When you have some of your equity in cash, you can use that to reinvest in another property or area.

While there are many positive aspects to refinancing, it is also important to consider the negatives while you are trying to make this decision. There are always risks involved when it comes to investing and finances. Since refinancing is essentially like taking out a new loan, you are agreeing to new loan terms and new loan amounts, and you will likely have to pay all the closing costs again. These costs cover fees, underwriting, title deed services, and appraisal. You might expect to pay somewhere between 3% and 6% of the balance of your loan for these closing costs.

Another thing that people don't often consider is the time and research you need to do in order to select the right loan and lender. This is similar to the process you would have undertaken when you first started looking for a loan for your property investment. You likely didn't jump into the first loan or mortgage you were offered, and you would have needed to do your research to ensure you were getting the best deal. The same principle applies here, so you need to be aware that you will need to invest a lot of time and effort. It is also important to understand that your credit score might take a hit because you are taking out a new mortgage. This will likely not last very long, but be prepared for a drop in your score that could last anywhere from a few months to a couple of years. This might not be all that bad, depending on what your credit score currently is.

It is important to understand your loan-to-value (LTV) ratio so that you can know how much you owe on your current mortgage relative to the value of your property. This is an essential ratio to grasp when you are trying to refinance your property. It can significantly impact your ability to secure a favorable interest rate on your new mortgage and may also determine your eligibility for certain loans. If your LTV is on the higher side, it will be more difficult for you to obtain a loan.

Calculating this number is relatively simple; all you need to do is divide the amount you currently owe on your mortgage by the value of your property and then multiply that number by 100. You will obtain a percentage, which will represent your LTV. Depending on the type of refinancing loan you intend to pursue, you might only need a percentage of 97% or lower to qualify (Kenton, 2023). However, for certain options, such as a cash-out refinance, you will need an LTV of about 80% (Parker, 2025).

When you are going through the refinancing process, it is important to ensure that you have all your ducks in a row and that all your documentation is ready to go. You can start collecting this information as early as possible to make the process smoother when you reach the refinancing stage. You will need proof of rental income, property appraisal, and renovation receipts, to name a few of the required documents. Additionally, you can contact your preferred loan provider to inquire about any other documentation they require, ensuring that you have everything on hand to facilitate the process.

SAFELY ACCESSING EQUITY

When you are following the BRRRR method, it is important to safely access equity with as little risk to yourself as possible. We have already mentioned the cash-out refinance, which is a great way to access equity safely. With a cash-out refinance, you will use the equity in your current property to access cash, allowing you to purchase another property. This is not a second mortgage, which means it is distinct from a traditional line of credit. Essentially, you are replacing your current mortgage with a new loan that will include the balance you owe on your current property plus the equity you are borrowing to make your next investment.

All the other benefits of refinancing are still available with a cash-out refinance. For example, if there are better interest rates now than there were when you first took out your mortgage, you will benefit from lowering your overall interest rate with your new loan. This is definitely the way to go when you are following the BRRRR method, and many investors have done the same.

While leveraging can be a great tool to help you make more money through diversifying your real estate investments, there is a risk of over-leveraging. When you over-leverage, you put yourself in more debt than you can handle, or the amount of debt you have on your property exceeds its current market value. This makes it difficult to recover your funds.

The good news is that over-leveraging can be avoided. If you do your research and ensure you conduct your due diligence before purchasing a property or taking out a mortgage, you can mitigate this risk. You need to understand all the expenses that will arise from purchasing the property so that you aren't taken by surprise and require a much higher loan than expected. This means you will need to comprehend the property's expenses right from the start. Once you do that, you should also ensure that your debt-to-equity ratio is less than 70% to make sure it is manageable and that you will have good leveraging power.

It is also good practice to stick to a few investment properties rather than trying your hand at multiple investments, as these can be difficult to manage. If you are a beginner, then just stick to one or two additional properties so that you can get a feel for the BRRRR method. Once you are comfortable, you can move on to more properties. Remember that real estate investing is not a get-rich-quick scheme, which means you will likely need to take your time to ensure that you aren't losing any money.

CALCULATING CASH FLOW AND SETTING RENTS

When you are ready to start renting out your property, it is important to set the right rent so that you are not selling yourself short or making less money than you possibly could. At the end of the day, you want to maximize your profits so you can increase your cash flow. This begins with researching how much others are charging for rent for comparable properties. Look for a property that is very similar to yours and located in the same area, and see what others are charging. This will give you a good indication of how much people are willing to spend in that area for your type of property. You can easily conduct this research by visiting property websites like Zillow and even Craigslist. Remember that you will likely be able to charge more money after you have made your improvements and renovations, so you can also hire a home appraiser to help you determine the value of the property and how much you can charge in rent if you are finding it difficult to locate comparable properties.

Another factor to consider is the laws in your area, as many regions have limits on landlords regarding how much they can charge for rent. This means that the amount you charge for rent may not be entirely up to you. Rent control laws are a very real consideration depending on the city, state, or country in which you live. You'll need to ensure that you understand these laws so that you're not violating them and becoming liable for repercussions.

You will also need to check for seasonality, which means that certain seasons or times of the year will have more demand for rental properties than others. A simple example would be if you are situated in a college town; it is more likely that you will find a renter during the school term, as that is when students will flock to the town and need a place to stay. During peak times, you'll be able to charge more for rent than when demand is much lower.

A common rule that you can use when determining how much you can charge for rent is the 1% rule. It is a simple calculation where you multiply the property's value by 1%. The number you obtain will be an estimate of what you can expect to charge for rent. However, this is a very rough estimate, so it is important to take into consideration other factors such as demand, location, and market conditions. This will provide you with a starting point, and then you can conduct further research to refine the amount you will be charging for rent.

EFFECTIVE PROPERTY MANAGEMENT

When it comes to managing your property, the first thing you need to do is ensure that you find the right tenant. Finding good and reliable tenants will make things much easier for you down the road. It means that you will have someone living in your property whom you can trust, making your income more reliable and ensuring that your property is well taken care of. This is why it is so important to take your time when looking for tenants and not rush the process just to fill the vacancy.

The first step is to advertise your rental property to get the word out that you have a vacancy. This is not as simple as quickly putting up an ad on a property website and hoping for the best. You want to put your best foot forward to attract high-quality potential tenants. Firstly, you need to understand who your target market is. Look at your property and consider who your ideal tenant would be. For example, if you have a studio apartment in the middle of a big city, your tenant will likely be a couple or a single person with a career who wants to be close to the city center. You can then tailor your advertising to this specific tenant. Highlight aspects that they would find important and what they are looking for in a place to stay. If your property is a larger home with a garden and is close to good schools, your target market might be a family with small children. In this case, you should emphasize safety, amenities, children's activities, space, and other factors that parents of young children would consider important. This is what your target audience is looking for, so when they search for something, you want to be at the top of the search results.

Putting your best foot forward in advertising your property also involves taking high-quality photos. One of the biggest mistakes I see people making is that the photos they take of their properties are so poor that they deter potential applicants. Ensure that you take photos when the lighting is good, and it is also a good idea to clean up the space to make it look appealing. You might want to hire a professional to help you take stunning pictures. Once you have your photos, you will also want to create a detailed listing that highlights all the positive aspects of your property to attract your target tenant.

You don't only have to advertise on property websites because social media is also a great tool. Additionally, people you know could spread the word, and it is more likely that you will find a good-quality tenant through word-of-mouth and your network than by sifting through thousands of applications from random individuals. Speaking of your network, it is always a good idea to broaden it by speaking to local real estate agents and attending real estate investment events. This way, you can build connections with people who could possibly help you find the right tenant for your property.

Once you have a few applicants, it is time to start the tenant screening process. This is where you conduct background checks and delve deeper into who your potential tenants are so that you can make the right choice. The screening process begins with the rental application. You'll need to have your potential tenant fill out an application and provide all of their basic information to get started. This information will include their name, contact information, employer, and rental history. Your potential tenant might also want to provide additional information to help you make your decision. To ensure that you are not overwhelmed with thousands of applications from individuals who would not qualify, you can set some applicant requirements in your advertisement to immediately disqualify those you would not consider. These minimum requirements could include a certain income level or credit score.

Now that you have all of your applicants' basic information, you can run some checks to ensure that you have good candidates. These checks will include credit history, rental history, and an overall background check. This is important because you want to get a clear idea of how financially responsible your potential tenant is, as well as their rental history, so that you can spot any red flags early on. You can also run a criminal history check if you wish. However, it is important to note that you cannot discriminate against someone based on their criminal history unless the crime is related to their past or present tenancy.

Once you have completed all of your screenings and background checks, you can review what you have learned about your potential tenants and then narrow down the applicants. Once you have a good number of quality applicants, you can conduct interviews to see if you get along with your prospective tenants or if there are any red flags that you might notice when speaking with them. It is a good idea to plan what you are going to ask them in advance so that you can accurately compare your potential tenants and ensure that you are asking the most important questions. If there is anything concerning that arose in your background checks, you can also ask them to elaborate, as there may be a valid reason for it, which could provide you with peace of mind.

There is a lot that goes into building a solid foundation for the BRRRR method. It is important to do this groundwork to ensure that whatever steps you take beyond this will have the best chance of leading you to success. In the next chapter, we will take some time to explore how incorporating short-term rentals can further enhance your rental income and investment returns.

FROM DREAM TO REALITY

"Every person who invests in well-selected real estate in a growing section of a prosperous community adopts the surest and safest method of becoming independent, for real estate is the basis of wealth."

— THEODORE ROOSEVELT

Everyone wants financial freedom, but the majority of people have no idea how to achieve it. To them, it will always be a dream—unless, that is, they see just how possible it is. I told you at the beginning of our journey together that I was unsure about real estate investing at first. To begin with, it was just about making sure my family had somewhere to live. It was only when I refinanced that house and used the equity to acquire another property that I realized what I could do with real estate investing.

Real estate is one of the most solid investments you can make, and the return you can get from it is, in most cases, far higher than it is for other forms of investment. I had to prove this to myself before I believed it, but now my goal is to help other people see just how possible it is. I talk to so many people who tell me that they're not wealthy enough to invest in property or that they don't even own their own house so they couldn't possibly consider it. They assume that these things are barriers, which means they don't even look into it.

I want to show people that there are fewer barriers to real estate investing than most people realize. I'm sure you've heard the expression, "Give a man a fish, and you feed him for a day. Teach a man to fish, and you feed him for a lifetime." That's how I view sharing what I know about real estate investment: I want to teach as many people as I can to build their wealth over their lifetime—and you can help me, simply by leaving a short review online.

By leaving a review of this book on Amazon, you'll help new readers to find it and understand that they, too, have the power to make money from real estate.

Anyone who's even slightly curious about whether they could make real estate investing work for them is looking for guidance—and your review will help them to find it. Together, we can help more people to make sure that financial freedom has a chance of becoming a reality instead of remaining a dream. I don't know about you, but that's a world I want to live in.

Thank you so much for your support. Now, let's get back to business!

Scan the QR code below

USING AIRBNB TO SUPERCHARGE RENTAL INCOME

The global short-term rental market is estimated to be worth $135 billion, reflecting a 9.7% increase from 2019 to 2023 (Achen 2025). This growth highlights the lucrative opportunities available to property owners who effectively leverage platforms like Airbnb. I have personally found success with Airbnb, which has far exceeded my expectations. Once I decided to truly get involved and create a plan, I was able to see significant financial gains through the Airbnb platform, and it is the reason I am so passionate about real estate.

WHEN AIRBNB IS A STRATEGIC CHOICE

When it comes to renting out your property, you don't have to do it solely on a long-term basis. A long-term strategy is great for many people, but you can definitely earn a substantial amount of money through Airbnb and short-term rentals. If you have never considered Airbnb as an option, let this be your sign to at least think about it.

Whether your Airbnb will be successful depends on several factors. Properties located in tourist-heavy areas or near major stadiums and events will have the highest chance of generating a steady income. Since Airbnb is a short-term rental strategy, the goal is to achieve higher occupancy rates, which means more people booking with you over time.

The type of property you have may not matter, as there are many different ways to rent out a property on Airbnb. It offers very flexible options, so you are likely to find one that is best suited to you. Firstly, you could rent out an entire standalone house. This means your guests will have access to the rooms, facilities, amenities, and anything else on the property. This arrangement is quite desirable, as guests enjoy having all the space to themselves, and it provides them with additional privacy.

You could also rent out an apartment or a condo in a larger building or complex. In this case, you would be renting out whatever is in that apartment, such as the rooms, living area, bathrooms, and kitchen. There will also be some shared areas and amenities, such as the laundry room, swimming pools, outdoor amenities, and entrances. Another option is to rent out a private room on Airbnb. This works if you have a space in your home that is not currently being used. Your guests will have their own private room, but they will need to share spaces like the living area, dining area, kitchen, and possibly the bathroom.

The final option is the shared room option, where one bedroom is shared by multiple guests. Think of a dormitory where several people sleep in one room using separate beds or bunk beds. There will also be shared rooms and amenities, such as the bathroom and kitchen. This will be a very affordable option for most guests, but it's not universally appealing, so only those who are on a budget would be attracted to something like this.

As you can see, there are many different options when it comes to renting out an Airbnb. Something good to know is that there are quite a few amenities that stand out from the crowd and make a property even more attractive on the Airbnb platform. Remember, people are booking with Airbnb because they're looking for a short-term rental, either for a vacation, business trip, or some other personal reason. In most cases, they are looking for a comfortable place to stay, and if they are on vacation, they will want some special amenities. A pool or hot tub is a great draw, and people will be willing to pay more for this. Staying with the water theme, if you have a property near the waterfront or with beach access, this is also a great draw. Everybody loves a view of the water, plus there are so many things to do, including water sports or even just relaxing on the beach. Water is not the only thing that attracts people; they also love outdoor and mountain views, so any of those options would be really good locations for an Airbnb.

If you have interesting architecture, a luxury bathroom, or unique amenities, such as a theater room, then these features will also attract more people. In the case of individuals wanting to book an Airbnb for business reasons, having an office space will be key and a significant attraction. What will attract your potential guests depends on their needs and your location. If you're situated in a city center or an economic hub, you are likely to attract more people who are coming to the city for work trips, and catering to them will be important. However, if you have a property that is more on the outskirts, where there are plenty of views, activities, and water attractions, you are likely to attract more people who are there for a vacation.

On Airbnb, you can also advertise experiences, not just property rentals. You can curate specific experiences in your area that potential guests would be excited to participate in, such as rides, city tours, sightseeing tours, and fun activities. You can add these experiences to your Airbnb booking package to make it even more attractive for people looking for a fun holiday experience. You can provide guests with tips and tricks for the area, as well as guide them to restaurants or provide maps of the area where they can go hiking, biking, swimming, or skiing. You might also be able to provide them with locations for museums and historical sites so they can explore while they're in the area. Remember that with Airbnb, you are essentially creating an experience rather than just renting out a place for people to stay. The more effort you put into creating a wonderful experience for your potential guests, the better your chances are of receiving positive reviews and more bookings.

Airbnb is a short-term rental platform, which means that when you engage with it, you'll be involved in short-term rentals. Short-term rentals require significantly more hands-on work and effort because you need to ensure that your guests are well taken care of, and you must prepare the property for the next guests after your current ones check out. There is indeed a lot that goes into managing an Airbnb, which is why I have written two books on this specific topic.

You can find both of my books on Amazon by scanning the QR code:

These books have already helped many people build the Airbnb business of their dreams, so I'm confident they will be useful to you if this is something you are considering as well.

Additionally, I have a Facebook community group specifically for Airbnb and short-term rental owners. This is a great place for people to connect and receive helpful tips and tricks along their Airbnb journey. Feel free to join this group to gain valuable insights and connect with others who are on the same journey as you.

Name: Airbnb Host Community

URL: https://www.facebook.com/groups/ airbnbhostcommunity

QR Code:

You can choose to have either a short-term or a long-term rental. Both options have their pros and cons, so it is better to understand these before you choose a strategy. Let's discuss them in more detail.

Short-Term Rentals

For most of this book, we have been discussing long-term rentals or at least considering them as an option. Now we are going to switch gears and talk about the pros and cons of short-term rentals so that you fully understand this method.

Pros

A significant advantage of short-term rentals is that they offer a lot of flexibility. You can decide when you want to rent your property out and when you want to keep it vacant or live in it yourself. For example, if you own a beach cottage that you want to use for family vacations a few weeks a year, you can rent that property out through short-term rentals during the times you are not going to be there. This way, your property does not remain vacant and unused for the majority of the year, but you still have the option to enjoy a vacation home when you want it. This flexibility also allows you to be much more hands-on with your property, enabling you to check and inspect it whenever you need to. This means you can conduct more frequent maintenance checks compared to if someone were living on your property on a long-term basis and would prefer not to be disturbed as often.

Short-term rentals also provide the opportunity to earn significantly more money than long-term rentals. Consider this: When you book a vacation, you pay per night. If you multiply the per-night rate at an average vacation rental by 30 days, this amount would be much greater than what someone would pay for monthly rent at the same property. If your property has a good booking rate, with people staying fairly often, you will definitely be making more money than if you were renting it out on a long-term basis.

Another major benefit is that you are far less likely to encounter legal disputes with a short-term rental than with a long-term one. Tenant rights and laws can lead to lengthy legal disputes, whereas in a short-term rental situation, the guest is only staying for a few days. They are unlikely to have the time to engage in any significant arguments or disagreements that could lead to legal action.

Cons

There are some downsides to short-term rentals that are important to be aware of. One of the biggest risks is the possibility of long vacancies for the property. You can never truly predict the market, and there is a chance that your property will not receive as many bookings as you would like. Additionally, you must take into consideration the seasonal market and the type of property you have. If you own a beach vacation home, it is likely that during the winter, there will be few people interested in booking with you. In this case, you might experience a season where you do not have any guests for months on end. There is also significant competition for short-term rentals, and if you have found a good area for an Airbnb, it is likely that other Airbnbs are in the vicinity.

Since different people are coming in and out of your property all the time, you must consider the fact that this could result in increased wear and tear on the amenities and the general structure of the property. It is also important to recognize that people might be a bit more careless while on vacation, so the chances of scuffs, scratches, and other minor damages could increase. You also need to remember that while you may have a certain standard for how you like to take care of things or live in a house, this standard may not be the same for other people. Spills, stains, and damage are all common and may require you to perform regular maintenance and refurbishment more often.

Another downside is the risk of neighbor complaints due to unruly or loud guests. Even if your guests are well-behaved, there may be inconveniences that you inadvertently cause your neighbors, such as parking congestion or a buildup of dirt and trash. Since your guests will be staying on a short-term basis, they may not be familiar with the norms of the neighborhood, which could lead to behaviors that irritate your neighbors.

With a short-term rental or an Airbnb, you do need a high level of involvement since there is a high turnover rate of guests. You'll have to ensure that the house is cleaned and restocked before your next guest checks in. On top of that, you might also need to be available should there be an issue that a guest needs help with. Remember that you are essentially providing a service to your guests, so being on call is simply part of the job. You want to make sure your guests have the best experience, and this means that you need to assist them when they need it. If not, they might leave a negative review, which could heavily impact your future bookings.

Another thing to consider is that maintenance is much more urgent with a short-term rental because you want to ensure your guests have the best quality stay and that their satisfaction level is high. If there are non-urgent or smaller maintenance tasks, you might be able to schedule them for a later date with a long-term rental, but this is not the case with a short-term rental. Additionally, you can't perform maintenance when your guests are on the property, as this will not go well for your ratings or your overall guest experience. This means that you might need to conduct maintenance by not taking any bookings for a certain period or by scheduling it outside of business hours, which might result in you paying higher fees for your contractors.

Long-Term Rentals

Let's have a look at some of the pros and cons of long-term rentals.

Pros

The huge benefit of a long-term rental is that the income stream is much more predictable. You and your tenant will agree on a rental amount that will be paid to you regularly, and you can expect this amount on a specific payday. This allows you to know how much money is coming in and to budget accordingly. This arrangement is a commitment between you and your tenant, and you can rely on this consistent payment.

Long-term tenants also tend to take better care of the property since they view it as a long-term stay and as their home. This creates a sense of ownership, and they feel responsible for the space. They are also likely to report any maintenance issues quickly so that they can be resolved before escalating into something bigger.

With a long-term rental, there is a lower likelihood of long vacancy periods, and the turnover rate is significantly smaller. This results in much less work for you because you don't have to market the property and find new tenants constantly. Additionally, your tenants will need to give you notice before they pack up and leave, which gives you some time to find new tenants.

Cons

There are a few downsides to long-term rentals that are important to consider. Firstly, there isn't much flexibility when it comes to your property. You won't be able to use your property for personal purposes until the lease agreement has ended. Your tenants have exclusive use of the property, and you have very little control over what occurs. Additionally, you need to respect your tenants' privacy, so you can't always check up on or inspect the property.

You also need to be well-versed in the legal landscape and tenant rights surrounding long-term rentals. If you have problematic tenants, they could use this to their advantage, which could disadvantage you and pose significant challenges. It can be very difficult to evict a tenant, even if they are not paying rent or taking care of the property. There are strict rules and guidelines that you must follow to address these situations, and it could take months or even years to achieve the desired outcome.

Another downside is that you may have to deal with problematic tenants, which can be incredibly time-consuming. Unlike short-term rentals, you don't get to restart with a new group of people after a few days. The issues that arise with long-term rentals stem from the fact that tenant and landlord relationships are much more complex, time-consuming, and resource-intensive. You may need to engage in extensive communication, problem-solving efforts, and negotiations. You might also need to involve other professionals, such as lawyers and property experts, to help resolve the issues. All of this can be incredibly time-consuming and expensive.

Airbnb and short-term rentals, in general, are great strategies for renting out your property to many people. There are some factors you need to consider to ensure that this is something you can handle. It might require significantly more time and effort on your part because you have to manage the property and ensure your guests are happy at all times. However, the positives and benefits are definitely worth it if you have the time and capacity to do this. You can potentially earn much more money with a short-term rental, plus you get the opportunity to meet a variety of interesting people from all around the world. It is crucial to assess your properties and the current market to determine if Airbnb is a suitable avenue for increasing your rental income. You could use Airbnb for one or two of your properties in your real estate portfolio while keeping the others as long-term rentals, allowing you to have a variety of income streams. Ultimately, it is up to you and the strategy you wish to pursue.

In understanding how Airbnb can boost your rental income, it's essential to establish a solid legal and financial foundation. This is important regardless of the rental strategy you use with the BRRRR method. In the next chapter, we will discuss the business structures, financial planning, and legal considerations necessary for long-term success in real estate investing.

PART III

BUILD SMART AND GROW BIG

LET'S TALK LEGAL, FINANCIAL, AND BUSINESS MATTERS

According to the IRS, all rental income must be reported on your tax return, and in general, the associated expenses can be deducted from your rental income (Internal Revenue Service n.d.). This is why it is important to know the ins and outs of legal and financial matters.

CHOOSING THE RIGHT OWNERSHIP STRUCTURE

Choosing the right ownership structure is crucial when you are investing in real estate. Your two main options are individual ownership or LLC ownership, which stands for limited liability company. With individual ownership, it is incredibly simple and involves owning the property in your name. There is less paperwork and administration required for this option. With an LLC, you separate your personal assets from your property or real estate investment. This means that should there be a lawsuit or claim against your property, your personal finances and wealth will be protected. It means that your investment is owned by a separate entity; even though you own that entity, you are not personally liable. If there is a claim or a lawsuit regarding your property, it will go through the LLC rather than your name. Basically, just as if an individual sues a company, the CEO of the company is not personally responsible for paying that claim out of his or her own pocket. It is covered by business expenses, and the business takes care of it separately from any personal assets.

Another thing to consider is the tax implications that come with both methods. When you own a property individually, you will need to file taxes on your rental income as part of your personal tax return. If your properties are under an LLC, there is a completely different way to file your taxes. The income you generate from your properties is not taxed at a corporate level, so you will need to file Form 1065 and then report the income on your individual tax return.

When it comes to how easy it is to use either of these methods, there are definitely advantages and disadvantages to both. For example, if you have the property under individual ownership, you can easily access funds from your bank or financial service provider without the additional work of setting up an LLC.

However, with an LLC, there are additional protections against creditors, plus you can establish a board of directors for better decision-making as your business grows. When you own a property in your personal capacity, there is no protection against personal liability, so you will have to take full responsibility if there is legal action, and your personal assets might be at risk of being repossessed if there are any financial issues.

UNDERSTANDING PERMITS, INSURANCE, AND CONTRACTS

When purchasing a property to renovate or improve, it is important to understand all of the permits and contracts that you will need in order to do so legally and safely. Undertaking these improvements without proper research can put you at risk of engaging in illegal activities, making you liable for fines or even jail time. It is also important to remember that most states and municipalities have different regulations, so you'll need to research your specific area to find out what permit contracts or legal frameworks are in place to ensure compliance. Although the permit process can vary from place to place, some basics are important to understand, regardless of where you live.

Not every small home improvement will require a permit, but larger projects that involve electrical, mechanical, and structural changes will likely need one. Any of these changes must comply with local codes, and you will need a basic plan in place before applying for a permit. Examples of projects that might require a permit include fencing, new windows, plumbing, electrical work, siding, water heaters, and renovations that exceed a certain total cost. Smaller tasks, such as painting, installing new walls, minor electrical work, new countertops, or adding fixtures and faucets, typically do not require a permit.

In addition to obtaining the necessary permits, you should also consider getting insurance to cover your property and renovations. At the end of the day, many things could go wrong, and you don't want to be out of pocket for any unexpected events. Having insurance will protect you and your property, ensuring that you have the funds available to handle emergencies. Unfortunately, there are many instances where an unexpected emergency occurs, and the property owner does not have enough money to address it. In such cases, the property owner may need to sell the property to mitigate their losses, or the property may remain in disrepair for years until the owner can save enough money to continue with the renovations. This results in wasted time and lost revenue, which is definitely something you want to avoid.

There are many different types of insurance available, and if you obtain general home insurance, it might be covered under that umbrella. Looking for some sort of umbrella policy might be your best option because it means that you only have to pay one insurance bill rather than multiple different insurance premiums. It is always a good idea to compare insurance premiums in terms of their cost and the benefits you will receive from them. You also want to ensure that the claims process is straightforward, so look for insurance providers that have good reviews and real-life examples of people being able to access their claims quickly.

As mentioned earlier, many things could go wrong when you own a property. The type of insurance you will obtain depends on the type of property you have as well as your location. In certain areas, there are greater risks for specific issues than in others. For example, some areas have a higher chance of flooding or fires, and in such cases, you want to ensure that your insurance policy covers these and other natural disasters. Other aspects you want your insurance policy to cover include liability, loss of income, and rent guarantee insurance. You should also consider obtaining insurance for workers' compensation and builders' risk insurance, especially if you are undertaking a larger project with many workers on-site. If something were to happen to the workers, you might be liable for their medical expenses, so having this insurance means that it will not come out of your pocket.

You also need to have the right contracts when you are involved in property investment or purchasing a property. There are many different types of contracts available, but there are five that you should consider, which are the most common in this context. The first is a purchase agreement, where the buyer and the seller agree to transfer ownership of a specific property. All the details regarding the sale and transfer of the property will be included in this contract.

The next common type of contract is an assignment contract. This is specifically for wholesaling, as it facilitates the property sale between the current homeowner and a separate buyer who is not the wholesaler.

Another contract is a lease agreement, which is a contract between the tenant and the landlord. This contract outlines the expectations of both parties, as well as the rent that the tenant needs to pay to the landlord.

Power of attorney is another important contract, necessary when the owner of a property grants permission for their attorney or another individual to act as their proxy in the transaction.

The final common contract is a subject-to contract. With this contract, the person buying the property will take over the seller's existing mortgage payment without needing to go through the entire process of obtaining their own mortgage, undergoing a credit check, or making a down payment.

TAXES AND RECORD-KEEPING

Whenever you are earning income, regardless of how or where it is coming from, you need to keep the taxes in mind. You must ensure that you are paying your taxes correctly; otherwise, you could face hefty fees and possible jail time if you are purposely avoiding paying taxes or evading the tax authorities. Unfortunately, taxes are a normal part of society, and we all have to comply, so making sure that we know what we are liable for will benefit us in the long term.

Rental income needs to be reported and taxed, so if you are using the BRRRR method, this is something you need to consider. This type of income is reported by you on Schedule E (Form 1040), though you might receive a Form 1099-MISC from your property manager if they collected rent on your behalf and are required to report it (Internal Revenue Service 2024). If you are filling out your taxes online, the program will automatically prompt you to complete the appropriate forms, such as Schedule E. It is typically a good idea to get someone with experience to assist you with your tax return, especially if you are not familiar with the process. This will help you avoid any mishaps and allow you to save money on your taxes.

Many categories are tax-deductible when you are working with real estate. This is a great benefit, and it's important to know what these deductions are so that you can effectively lower your taxable income and the amount of taxes you will be paying. Some expenses that can be deducted include mortgage interest, property tax, operating expenses, depreciation, and repairs.

It is very important that you keep thorough records of your income, expenses, and any financial transactions related to your property. This will help you with your tax filing process and allow you to analyze your finances. It is recommended that you keep a record for at least three years. You may choose to keep your financial and tax records for longer, just in case, but this is definitely the minimum. When you maintain a record of all your income and expenses, it will make tax preparation much easier because you will have everything on hand. If the IRS requests certain proof or documentation, you can quickly provide it, which will reduce the amount of time you spend going back and forth. It also makes the process significantly less stressful.

In general, you must have documentary evidence, including items such as checks, bills, receipts, and emails that can support your expenses. A good rule of thumb is that if you have spent any money on or for your property, you should keep the evidence of this safely. You can retain hard copies, but you can also scan or take pictures of the hard copies and save them digitally, making it easier to keep track of what you have. Additionally, you can keep a record of any travel expenses related to rental property repairs. You may want to consult a tax professional to find out if there are any other tax deductions you could qualify for. Although hiring a tax professional does incur a cost, they are usually worth it because they can make your life much easier and save you money in the long run by helping you reduce your tax liability.

SETTING UP BUSINESS ACCOUNTS AND SYSTEMS

It is not necessarily mandatory, but it is a good idea to set up separate bank accounts for your property business and your personal account. While it might seem like a tedious process to establish these different accounts, it will definitely be worth it in the long run, as it simplifies your finances and makes tax season much easier for you.

There are numerous benefits to having a separate account for your business or property investments. One is that it prevents the co-mingling of funds. It is easy to let your business and personal funds become mixed, making it difficult to determine which goes where, especially if everything is in one account. When everything is combined, it can be very challenging to track your expenses and report them for financial and tax purposes. Having a clear separation between your accounts simplifies everything, allowing you to prevent overspending in certain areas. It also helps protect your personal assets and funds.

When you have a separate account, your general accounting for your rental property will be much easier because you can easily track your income and expenses. If you need to review your spending, you can be confident that the expenses in your property account are solely for your property and nothing else. This will reduce the overall preparation time when you are preparing for taxes and financial accounting in general.

As your portfolio grows and you acquire more properties, having a separate bank account makes managing your finances significantly easier. You can also establish a separate bank account for each of your properties, allowing you to track how well each one is performing. This will also be beneficial when you apply for financing from lenders, should you wish to refinance a property or purchase another one.

As your portfolio grows, you might want to start hiring people to assist you with certain areas of your business. This could include property management, accounting, or general administrative duties. These individuals will then become part of an employee payroll, and it will be much simpler if there is a separate account from which you pay these employees. You will also be able to pay your vendors from this account, ensuring that you do not overspend in that area. You will know exactly how much money is in your account, how much you have to spend, and what you need to budget for.

In addition to having these separate accounts, you can also utilize accounting software to help automate and streamline financial management. These days, we really do not have to do all the tedious work ourselves; we can use software and apps to assist. This makes everything much easier and provides us with additional insights that might be more difficult to obtain if we were doing everything on our own. Some good options include QuickBooks, AppFolio, Stessa, and Buildium.

BUILDING YOUR REAL ESTATE TEAM

As your real estate portfolio grows, you can't do everything on your own. It becomes incredibly important to bring people onto your team to help you focus on the things that really matter. Additionally, it is always a good idea to seek advice and assistance in various areas of property management and investing. There are many different roles you fill as a real estate investor, and outsourcing some of this workload will greatly assist you in balancing your tasks.

You might not be able to hire people for every single step of the process at the beginning, but you can always start somewhere and build your team as you progress. One of the first individuals or groups you can bring on board is a driver. This is not someone who will drive you around, but rather someone who will help you find properties that meet your investment criteria. This approach provides you with more options, increasing your chances of finding the right property.

The great thing about this role is that you don't necessarily have to hire a professional to fulfill it. When you first start out, consider reaching out to friends and family members who could be your initial drivers. All you need to do is inform them that you are looking for a specific property that meets your ideal criteria. If they are on the lookout for such properties, they can funnel any leads they find to you, allowing you to decide whether to pursue those options. As you continue your real estate investing journey, you will be able to recruit more drivers who will help you maintain a pipeline of potential property investments.

The next person you can bring on board is called a lead manager. This individual will take the leads provided by the drivers and call around to find the most qualified leads. They will gather more information about the properties that have come their way to identify which ones will be the best fit for you and your goals. It is important for this person to have good interpersonal skills, as they will be interacting with many people while discovering more about the properties.

You might also need an acquisitions manager, who is responsible for closing deals and acquiring the properties. They will receive information from the lead manager and then analyze the properties to determine how much you can offer. They need to possess excellent negotiation skills as well as a solid understanding of the real estate market. This knowledge will help them make better deals and understand what is realistic. The next step involves someone called a disposition manager, who handles the sale of the property after you have flipped and revamped it. They will work to sell your property to a list of qualified buyers to ensure that the sale goes through quickly. If you are not looking to sell the property, then you do not specifically need this person.

Another key member of your team would be a marketing manager or a marketing lead. Since you are on the hunt for new properties and also trying to sell your current properties, marketing will be crucial. Marketing can require a lot of time and effort, especially if you have multiple properties. They will assist by designing your marketing initiatives and working on strategies and plans to help promote your properties. They will also play a key role in attending networking events and conferences to meet more people who could potentially bring in additional leads.

On top of what we have just discussed, there are some other really important members of your team that you will need to get on board. This will include a lender who will provide you with funds while you are in the property market and looking to purchase properties. While you can apply for loans and go through banks and other avenues, having a lender or someone you know you can work with easily will greatly improve the process. Mutual trust will allow things to go more smoothly. If you have a designated person you know you can approach when you need a loan or some extra money, it will be beneficial.

You will also need a real estate agent to assist you with buying and selling properties, as well as a contractor who will help with building and renovating your property. Another important person will be an accountant who will handle the financial and tax aspects.

Some honorable mentions in terms of people you might want on your team include property managers who will manage the day-to-day operations of your property if you cannot do it yourself. They will handle the tenants and the individuals who work on the property daily, so you do not have to be on-site all the time. You might also want to consider getting an appraiser, inspector, or real estate attorney on board. Finally, consider hiring an insurance agent you can trust to help you obtain the best insurance products.

A lot goes into being an investor in real estate, and it's important to have all the finer details sorted out as soon as possible. You'll need to establish an appropriate ownership structure, understand the legal requirements, and maintain accurate financial records to ensure that your business is running at its optimum capacity. You might also want to bring on more people to assist you in areas where you may not be fully competent or where you simply need help. Once you have all of these in place, it will form a foundation for the next step, which is considering how you want to exit your investments effectively. This is exactly what we will be discussing in the next chapter.

EXIT STRATEGIES AND LONG-TERM PLANNING

Current data from CBRE and NCREIF indicates that over 68% of real estate investors in Q1 2025 revised their exit strategy within 18 months of acquisition (The Luxury Playbook 2025). This highlights the importance of having an exit strategy and adapting it to ensure that it remains effective in the current market and your specific situation. The real estate market is constantly changing, which means we sometimes need to be flexible with our plans regarding the properties we purchase. You might have acquired a property for a specific reason, such as renting it out, but upon further inspection and additional research, you may discover that this is not a renter's market. Consequently, you might need to sell your property or consider another strategy to profit from your investment.

TO SELL OR REFINANCE

When you are involved in real estate investment, you have a choice between mortgage refinancing and selling the property. Both options come with their own pros and cons, so it is important to understand your goals and what you hope to achieve. You also need to assess the housing market to determine which option will suit you better. While refinancing may have been your original plan, you might come to realize that selling could offer more benefits. It is always best to keep an open mind when investing in real estate, as circumstances can change, and you want to be flexible enough to achieve the best results.

Mortgage Refinancing Pros and Cons

When you refinance your property, you are essentially replacing your current mortgage with a new one. The monthly payment you make will now be applied to the new mortgage. There are many different refinancing options available, each with varying rates and terms. If you are using the BRRRR method, you will need to refinance your properties at some point. There are definite benefits to refinancing, including a lower interest rate, debt consolidation, and the opportunity to make home improvements.

When you refinance, you also have to take into consideration a few negatives or drawbacks that come with it. For example, you need a good credit score in order to secure a favorable rate on your refinance. If not, you will find it very difficult to obtain a new loan, which might even end up costing you more money. If you take a cash-out refinance, this can lower the equity in your home, which can be a significant disadvantage, especially if overall housing market prices decrease. Finally, another major downside to consider is that refinancing extends your debt timeline, meaning that you will need to pay back money for a longer period than you might have initially anticipated.

Selling Pros and Cons

Selling your home is another option you can explore. There are many reasons you might choose to sell your property, even if you are currently trying to implement the BRRRR method. This could be because you realize that the home is not generating the amount of money you expected, or perhaps you have too many properties in your portfolio, making it difficult for you to manage them.

One of the biggest benefits of selling your house is that you gain access to immediate funds as soon as the sale goes through. You receive a lump sum, and then you can do what you wish with that money. It also allows you to reduce your overall debt because you can sell your house, pay off your debts, and then take the profit from the sale. If you have owned your property for a significant amount of time or have improved it to the point where it has increased in value, you can sell your house for a much larger profit margin.

The downsides of selling your house include market-dependent value. This means that, because the housing market is always fluctuating, if you choose to sell your house when the market is low, you will receive a lower price than what you deserve or desire. Another factor to consider is that you will need to have your home reappraised if you want to sell, and this comes with additional costs. Selling also means dealing with uncertain timelines. Sometimes houses sell in a matter of days, while in other cases, it can take months or even years to sell. If you're looking to make quick money from selling your property, this may not be possible depending on the current market demand.

There are many reasons people choose to sell rather than rent, even if they are following the BRRRR method. Life can be unpredictable, and it's important to adjust your goals or priorities accordingly. For example, if you have financial goals and have determined that refinancing will not help you achieve them, then selling might be the better option. Perhaps your rental property is not generating much income, making it less worthwhile to keep. In cases where you co-own property with someone else and there is a death, divorce, separation, or a general partnership dispute, it might be better to sell so that everyone can recoup their investment rather than attempting to maintain a joint rental. Another reason people consider selling is if there is a significant issue with the property that will require too much time and resources to resolve. As you can see, there are many reasons to sell your property, and it all depends on your current situation and your goals.

UTILIZING 1031 EXCHANGES AND UNDERSTANDING TAX IMPLICATIONS

A 1031 exchange is a process that allows an investor to defer capital gains tax when selling an investment property. This is permitted because the proceeds are reinvested into another property that is very similar to the one being sold. Essentially, it is a swap from one property to another. While this may sound like an excellent idea since you do not have to pay the capital gains tax immediately, the truth is that it can be very difficult to find a similar property to the one you currently own. You also need to ensure that the new property is located in an area you like and meets all your other requirements, even if it is similar and qualifies.

There are some timing rules that come into play with the 1031 exchange. The first is the 45-day rule, which indicates that once the property has been sold, the intermediary entity will receive the money. As the seller, you will not be able to accept the cash immediately; otherwise, it will jeopardize the 1031 treatment. Within the 45 days, you must designate the property you are replacing your current one with in writing. You can designate up to three properties, as long as you intend to close on one of them. In some cases, you may designate more than three. The other rule is the 180-day rule, which requires you to close on your new property within 180 days after selling your previous property. You can also purchase a replacement property before selling the one you currently own and still qualify for this exchange, but the same 45- and 180-day time windows will apply.

If you engage in a 1031 exchange, you will need to report this to the IRS. You must submit Form 8824 along with your tax return for the year in which the exchange occurred. In this form, you will need to provide descriptions of both properties, the dates they were transferred, and your relationship with the person or people with whom you exchanged properties. You will also need to indicate the value of each property.

One important tax implication to be aware of is depreciation recapture. This occurs when the IRS collects tax on the depreciation you claimed after selling your assets for more than their book value. Within this category, there are two types of properties you might need to calculate: 1245 property and 1250 property.

Using Section 1245 property includes the depreciation of the property when calculating the profit from its sale. Let's say you bought a property for $100,000, and each year you claim $10,000 as depreciation deductions, which means you are lowering your taxable income by $10,000 every year. After five years, you would have claimed $50,000, making your adjusted cost basis $50,000. This is because you subtracted the amount you have deducted over the five years from the original cost. Let's say that in this scenario, the housing market is really bad, and when you sell your property, you sell it for only $70,000. This might seem like a loss because you originally spent $100,000 on the property when you first bought it, but the IRS calculates things differently. Instead of comparing it to the original sale price, they adjust the value of the property based on the deductions. So, if the new value is $50,000 and you sold it for $70,000, it means that you have made a $20,000 profit. That $20,000 is subject to depreciation recapture, which means that you will be paying your regular income tax rate on that amount.

The next topic we will cover is Section 1250 gains. With this, the real estate investor benefits from a favorable depreciation recapture, as business equipment is taxed separately at a regular income rate, while real estate depreciation recapture is capped at 25%. To qualify for this, you will need to use straight-line depreciation. This means you will need to claim equal deductions every year over the lifespan of your property. When it comes time to sell your property and you sell it for more than the original price, the final sale price will be divided into two parts. The profit you make up to the amount of depreciation you've already claimed in previous years is subject to a maximum recapture rate of 25%. The profit that exceeds the original purchase price will be taxed at a lower long-term capital gains rate, which is around 15% for most people.

Speaking of capital gains, it is important to understand what they are and how they impact your taxes. Capital gains tax is simply the tax imposed on the profit after you have sold your property or any other asset. You have made gains from your investment, and those gains need to be taxed as profit since they qualify as income. Using the 1031 exchange is a good way to lower your capital gains tax, but there are also other strategies, including converting your second home into your main residence or investing in Opportunity Zones, which are designated areas that offer tax benefits for real estate investors. It is always a good idea to consult with an accountant or tax practitioner to help you minimize the amount you will pay in capital gains tax so that you can save as much money as possible.

BUILDING A SUSTAINABLE REAL ESTATE PORTFOLIO AND SCALING UP

As you continue on this real estate journey, you will want to ensure that you are building a sustainable real estate portfolio— something that lasts for a long time and continues to generate income. A strong portfolio will help establish a solid financial foundation for you, even in the face of changes in the housing market.

When building your real estate investment portfolio, it is important to have a long-term perspective so that you can set your objectives and goals correctly. Doing this will help streamline your choices as you begin to build your portfolio. You must know where you are going before you start taking steps to get there. Consider factors such as how much time you can dedicate to your real estate investment portfolio and the amount of work or effort you are willing to invest.

Once you know what you want to achieve from your real estate investing, it's time to choose a starting point. For first-time investors, it is crucial not to try to do too much at once. Even if you have the finances to invest in multiple properties, it is best to start small so that you can acclimate to real estate investing and understand its implications for your lifestyle. Starting small also allows you to gain a good understanding of real estate before committing to something larger. You might consider options like house hacking, as it is easier to qualify for a loan in this scenario and can help you pay off the main property in which you reside.

The next step is to consider how you will grow your portfolio. While it may seem appealing to expand your portfolio annually by continuously adding properties, exponential growth is far more advantageous. It demonstrates a greater increase over time. Linear growth involves investing in rental properties of the same or similar value every few years; while this approach will yield growth, it may take some time before you see anything substantial. However, if you create a portfolio that grows exponentially, you can use your rental income to leverage and accumulate more equity, allowing you to purchase additional properties that generate more income. This is the beauty of the BRRRR method. It enables you to leverage your investments and increase your income over time. Consequently, you will be able to acquire more properties in a shorter period, resulting in significantly higher profits.

If you want to have an edge in the real estate game, it is essential that you fully understand your local real estate market. This is especially important while you are still growing your real estate portfolio. If you are considering purchasing properties that are very far away from you, the truth is that you don't always know what's happening in your rental home or what is going on in the neighborhood. This poses challenges when you are trying to make decisions about your real estate investments, and there may be things that you are missing. If you keep your real estate investments in areas that you know well and can easily travel to, it will be much easier for you to keep track of things and ensure that you are getting the most out of your real estate investment. It is also easier to monitor your local market because you are there, and it will interest you since it impacts you personally, not just in your investment space.

As your real estate investment portfolio starts to grow, it is crucial to understand that diversification is key. When you diversify your real estate investments, you essentially protect yourself while maximizing your returns. A non-diversified portfolio is one in which you are only investing in one type of real estate or property. For example, you might only invest in apartments that are close to the city center. When you diversify, you spread your investment across different types of properties and locations. This is important because if something were to happen with one type of investment or property, it would not impact your entire portfolio as severely, since you have many different types within your portfolio. In the example where you own three apartments in the city center, if something were to happen to the city and it no longer becomes a popular place to live, you would essentially lose your revenue from all three of your investments. However, if you invest in a multifamily home in the suburbs, one apartment in the city, and an Airbnb vacation rental, even if something happens to the apartment in the city, the other two investments in your portfolio will still be generating income, so you will remain secure.

A good rule of thumb for diversification is the 60/20/20 rule. This is where you have 100% of your portfolio divided into three smaller categories. You can split it up however you like, but traditionally, 60% of your portfolio is allocated to multifamily residential properties, 20% goes to vacation rentals, and the last 20% is for private equity real estate funds. With this kind of diversification, you get the best of all worlds in real estate investing. You invest in long-term and short-term real estate, as well as funds, all of which have different levels of profit generation and security. You don't have to stick to these ratios, and it's best to find something that works best for you, but this is definitely a great starting point as you try to diversify your investment portfolio.

COMMON MISTAKES TO AVOID

There are many mistakes that you could make or be making when investing in real estate. Understanding these common mistakes early can help you avoid them as you move through this journey. If you know to expect something that could cause a problem down the line, you will recognize it quickly, and you might not have to deal with it at all. Let's talk about some of the most common mistakes when it comes to real estate investing.

Underestimating Costs

Underestimating the total cost of a house flip or rental is a very common mistake. It is easy to miscalculate the overall costs of renovating a house if you have not done it before. There are many things you might not think about until you reach the point where you need them. This is why it is important to conduct thorough research. You can also obtain quotes and appraisals to ensure you know what the costs will be. Then, you'll need to create a detailed budget and do your best to stick to it throughout the process.

Not Doing Enough Research

Research is a crucial step when you are going to invest a significant amount of your money in something. If you don't conduct your research properly, it could lead to bigger issues down the road. For example, if you don't research the city or area you are buying in and that area is in decline, you could end up unable to sell or rent out your property for as much as you would like when the time comes. Remember to conduct market research as well as research on contractors, materials, and anything else you might think is necessary.

Choosing the Wrong Location

When it comes to property, location will always be one of the most important factors to consider. People typically want to move to a specific area and then look for their dream house; it's not the other way around. Finding an area that is safe, clean, and easily accessible is crucial. You also want to ensure that the neighborhood has increasing or stable property values, as this improves your chances of getting the amount you want when you sell your property. If you can find an up-and-coming neighborhood or area, it will be a great benefit to you because it means you can buy at a lower rate and have a greater chance of making a profit.

Over-Improving the Property

Yes, there is such a thing as over-improving your property. This means that you are making more improvements than are necessary to achieve a good profit. Certain improvements will yield a good return on investment, while others, although nice, are not as worthwhile. When you are making an investment, every step you take needs to be aligned with your end goal. You want to maximize your profit while minimizing your expenses. This is not about cutting corners; rather, it is about being smart with your money to ensure that you are making worthwhile changes.

Rushing the Process (Timeline)

We all want to get things done as quickly as possible, but when it comes to real estate, it is not advisable to rush the process. This is especially true when renovating your property. Rushed work can lead to mistakes and problems that will cost you significantly to fix down the line. Quality will always be more important than speed. While you do not want things to be delayed unnecessarily, taking your time with each step is crucial to ensure that you are doing everything thoroughly.

Not Having an Exit Strategy

It is essential to have an exit strategy because you do not want to hold on to a property longer than necessary or end up selling it for a much lower price than you intended. Lost profit can lead to larger financial problems, especially if you have a strict budget or specific financial goals to achieve. Before purchasing a house to flip, make sure you have considered an exit strategy. This could involve selling the property if you are unable to find the right tenant, or if you have flipped the property and cannot find buyers, you might consider renting it out for some income. This way, you have a backup plan in case things do not work out as you had planned.

Not Enough Patience

A true professional is someone who takes their time to wait for the right property and the right buyer. It can be very tempting to rush through things, but this is not a good long-term strategy. Just because a house is cheap and the current owners appear desperate to sell does not mean that it will be a good buy for you. Remember to practice patience and take a breather between big decisions so that you know you aren't rushing into things.

It is crucial to understand your investment strategies and to reevaluate them from time to time to ensure they remain relevant in the current environment and real estate market. Consider implementing a few of the methods and suggestions we have discussed in this chapter to help you grow your investment business sustainably. Long-term planning is essential, and the next step is to put all of your knowledge into action. In the next chapter, we will discuss executing your first real estate investment deal to set your future up for success.

YOUR FIRST DEAL

My first deal wasn't anything flashy or massive. We were new immigrants, so we did not have a lot of disposable income to purchase the best properties in desirable areas. We bought an old, rundown house in the countryside because it was all we could afford. My wife and I had a newborn baby, and I had started a new job, so there was a lot we were still trying to figure out. The house needed a lot of work, but we were ready to roll up our sleeves and do most of the renovations ourselves. This included tasks such as installing new floors, building a new kitchen and laundry room, painting, replacing the doors, and land-scaping the garden.

My little family lived in this house for two years before we decided to get the property revalued. I originally bought the house for $282,000 and paid a 20% deposit. The rest was financed through a mortgage. Once the property was revalued, it was worth $345,000, which meant we had gained quite a bit of equity in just two years. From there, I decided to refinance and was able to borrow up to 80% of the new value. This meant I could borrow $276,000. The refinance replaced the original mortgage and gave us about $50,000 in cash-out equity. This amount was perfect for a deposit on a two-bedroom apartment, and we still had some money left over, so we decided to refinish the apartment and run it as a short-term rental. This marked the true start of my real estate investing journey and how I got into Airbnb.

If I'm being honest, those first couple of years didn't truly feel like I was making a real estate investment. I was just trying to make the best of my situation by improving the home where I lived. This hard work really paid off and became a catalyst for my real estate investment journey. My family and I took the first step and started small. We learned as we went along and chose to reinvest whatever we earned. These small steps made a huge difference in the long run. I gained momentum, and I used this to keep going. Eventually, my property portfolio grew one deal at a time. I know that if I hadn't taken that first step with my very first house and then purchased that apartment, I would never be where I am today. One smart move in the right direction is all it takes to change the entire game.

STAYING MOTIVATED WHEN DEALS GO WRONG

Even with the best-laid plans, a deal can still go wrong, or the market might not work in your favor. Even people who have been in the real estate game for decades can go through seasons when things are just not working out for them. You will likely face challenges for many reasons; some of them will be within your control, while others won't be. Regardless, it is essential to keep yourself motivated during hard times.

The first thing you need to do is control the things that you can. When things are not working out the way you wanted them to, it is important to understand what you can change and what you can't. If you have made a mistake or miscalculation, this is something you can fix going forward, and you don't have to deal with this bad patch for too much longer. For example, take a look at all of your listings and see if you are overpricing them for the market. Remember that the market changes all the time, and just because something has historically worked does not mean it will continue to do so forever. You might need to adjust your pricing strategy to attract more people to your properties.

It is also a good idea to examine your listings and see if there are any issues that are making them hard to sell. This might relate to how your listings are marketed or to the properties themselves. Perhaps there is something that is dissuading people from renting or buying from you. Put yourself in the shoes of a potential renter or buyer and view things from their perspective. You can even ask a friend, family member, or a completely impartial third party to review your listings and see if anything stands out as a red flag. If you identify any issues, you can make the necessary changes to make your listings more attractive.

Let's say you have checked your properties and have done all the work to ensure that your listings and properties are as attractive as possible. However, you are still not receiving the interest you had hoped for. In this case, it could simply be a rough patch, and it's something you just have to ride out until the market picks up and you can gain momentum once again. If you've been in the real estate game long enough, you will quickly notice that there will be a few times when you encounter these rough patches, and all you need to do is stay motivated until the wave is over. Things will definitely pick up again and return to normal, or even improve beyond normal.

While you're waiting for things to return to an optimal level for your investments, you can work on your mindset. The first step toward cultivating a more positive mindset is to figure out your "why." You've probably heard something along these lines before, but it's such a key part of anything you are trying to achieve. The goal is to uncover the deep reasoning behind your decision to embark on this journey in the first place. Sometimes, it can be easy to forget why we are doing something when we are in the thick of a problem. Reflecting on the beginning, when you first started, will help reawaken some of that passion and fire. Perhaps you wanted to start real estate investing to become financially free or independent. Maybe you want to create a better life for your family and children. Or perhaps you want to have enough money to retire early. Whatever your reasoning or your "why," write it down and keep it with you so that you have something to refer back to each day or when things get difficult.

The next thing you need to do is avoid any negativity from people who are either not in the field or who are simply glass-half-empty types. Whenever you are trying to achieve something great, there will always be individuals who have their own biases and negativity that they want to share with you. Such negativity can easily derail you and make you think the situation is far worse than it actually is. If there are negative people around you, it is an indication that you should not share your strategies or struggles with them. Of course, it is important to have people with whom you can bounce around ideas, but if someone is merely negative and not helping you find solutions, then that person is not the right ally for you. You don't have to cut them off completely, but you should distance yourself from them regarding your real estate investments and that aspect of your life. It is important to find someone who is positive and uplifting in that space to help you stay motivated and keep moving forward.

It might also be worthwhile to examine your current goals and see if they are realistic for where you are right now. If you are feeling like a failure, it could be that your goals do not align with the reality of your situation, making you feel worse than you should. By reevaluating your goals and making them a bit more realistic, you will feel as though you are making progress and actually reaching them, rather than feeling that you keep falling short.

Remember that anyone who has achieved greatness in any sphere of life has faced challenges. Challenges are completely normal, and they can provide a great learning experience if you allow them to. You may be in a difficult situation right now, but you will push through and emerge stronger on the other side if you keep going and maintain a positive outlook. You can look at other people's success stories to see how they have overcome struggles and what they did to build themselves up when times were tough. As you read about others' real estate investment journeys, you will quickly notice that everyone encounters some sort of bump in the road or challenge. Mindset is everything when it comes to reaching your goals and finding success.

THE 90-DAY ACTION PLAN

Having a 90-day plan will provide you with structure, allowing you to clearly work toward your first deal. This plan will serve as a guideline to help you take action. It can be all too easy to read something in a book and, once you reach the final page, fail to apply the information you have learned. A solid plan will help you move forward and allow you to see results. You can modify this action plan as you see fit, but make sure to create a plan for yourself and stick to it. You will find that you learn much more about real estate and investing simply by being active in the field.

Month 1

In the first month, the focus will be on research and analysis. This is what we discussed in the first part of this book. Feel free to revisit that section for a refresher on how to take action during the research and analysis phase. In this phase, you will do your best to thoroughly research the different types of investing and decide which one you want to pursue. Consider writing a pros and cons list tailored to your situation to help you determine which real estate investment strategy aligns with your goals and lifestyle.

You can further deepen your understanding of what you have already learned in this book by researching online and exploring the opinions of others. If you have joined my Airbnb Facebook group, you can ask for advice there or simply read what others have to say and see how you can apply it to your own plan or strategy. Additionally, you can attend real estate investing seminars or networking events to enhance your knowledge and skills, as well as to meet others in the same field.

It is also a good idea to create a simple matrix that includes several factors. You will use this matrix to compare each investment style, helping you understand which one is best suited for you. You can include as many factors as you like, but the four recommended factors are the pros of the strategy, the cons of the strategy, the minimum investment required, and the time commitment involved. Once you have completed this matrix, you can start comparing and identifying which option best suits your needs.

	Pros	Cons	Minimum Investment Needed	Time Required
Strategy 1				
Strategy 2				
Strategy 3				
Strategy 4				

Month 2

In month two, it is time for you to choose your tools. It is important that you select the right ones because, as they say, a builder is only as good as his tools. Choosing the right tools to work with will make your life much easier and more efficient. They will need to align with your overall goals and strategy.

Since there are so many tools available, it is essential for you to conduct some comparisons to help you make a decision. You can also create a matrix to compare different factors and then decide from there. Again, you can include as many factors as you deem fit, but the following are recommended: features, upfront investment, recurring investment, learning curve, and potential ROI.

	Features	Upfront Investment	Recurring Investment	Learning Curve	Potential ROI
Tool 1					
Tool 2					
Tool 3					
Tool 4					

Once you have completed the tools matrix, you will need to choose which ones you want to pursue. You do not need to have a large variety; rather, pick a few that will truly make the biggest impact on your real estate investment journey. You can always add more to your list as your portfolio grows or as you need them. Many tools require you to pay some kind of subscription, so you don't want to commit to too many while you are still in the beginning stages. Reach out to people who have a similar investment style and see if they have any recommendations, and ask how they use them. Also, remember to give yourself some time to learn how to use these tools effectively and navigate any of the platforms you will be using. Some have a steeper learning curve than others, so don't forget to allow yourself that time to learn before you need to use them.

Month 3

In the third month, you will be making your very first deal. This is where the rubber meets the road, and you will do your best to make your first investment. You have all the information from your research and your tools, so now it is time for you to get moving and try to close a deal. With the BRRRR method, the goal is to find a property to purchase so that you can renovate it and then rent it out. At this stage, you need to be on the hunt for the right property. This might mean getting on the phone and making calls or scouring the internet to see what your options are. You might even need to jump in your car and drive around your neighborhood to see what is actually happening in the area and if any potential properties catch your eye.

Commit to doing something each day toward meeting your goal. This way, you maintain momentum and ensure that you don't lose what you have built up. Make notes about what you are doing and how it is turning out for you. For example, if you are pursuing the right property, start writing down exactly what is being said and how you are being received by others. Making these notes is crucial at the beginning because it will help you identify patterns that may or may not be working, allowing you to change your approach or lean into a positive aspect.

You may not close your very first deal within the 90-day or three-month period, and that is completely okay. The goal of having this plan in place is to provide you with something to work toward and to help you build the habit of taking action. Once you reach the end of your 90 days, reevaluate your plan and assess how far you have come. You may have closed a deal, or you may not have; if you have, that's fantastic! If you did not manage to close a deal or find the right property, it doesn't mean you have to go all the way back to the drawing board. You can simply review your journal as well as the matrix you used while researching and discovering. This will provide in-depth information to help you make better decisions in the future and possibly create a more effective strategy.

Real estate investing is an exciting journey, and now that you have reached this point, you have a clear action plan. Congratulations! This is where things start to happen, and you get to see your knowledge transform into action. At this point, you are equipped to begin your real estate investing journey, and you are at one of the most exciting moments in your life. Real estate changed my life, and I'm sure it will do the same for you.

SHARE THE OPPORTUNITY!

Your journey is just beginning, but you still have a chance to help others out on theirs. If you take just a few minutes to leave a short review, you'll help them find it and launch their adventure with real estate investments.

Simply by sharing your honest opinion of this book and a little about your own experience, you'll inspire new readers to try it out for themselves—and you'll show them exactly where they can find all the information they need to get started.

JUST ONE CLICK!

Thank you so much for your support. I wish you every success in your ventures.

Scan the QR code to leave a review.

CONCLUSION

When I first started out as a young real estate investor, I don't think I fully understood how much it was going to change my life. I had seen other people invest in real estate, and it was something that definitely piqued my interest. However, I did not know where to start. It took me a long time to find my footing, and eventually, I began to gain traction. The more I engaged in it, the more I developed a passion for real estate investing. Then the BRRRR method came along, and I knew that this was something I needed to get involved in.

This is probably where you are in your journey. It's the exciting beginning phase, where there is so much opportunity and possibility in front of you. It is time for you to harness this feeling and the knowledge you have already gained from this book and take steps forward to build a better future for yourself and your family. Regardless of what your goals are, investing in real estate is a powerful tool to help you achieve them. Keeping the end goal in mind is what will keep you motivated as you progress through your real estate investment journey.

Remember that, regardless of what you do, the most important thing is to build a solid foundation. Learning, researching, and absorbing as much knowledge as you can is a crucial step. This will help you create a solid plan as you move forward with your investments. It will also enable you to recognize any red flags or potential problems because you have this knowledge tucked away in your memory bank. Even though it might not be the most exciting part of the process, it is crucial, and you shouldn't skip it. One challenge I like to set for myself is to read one article or watch one video about real estate investing every day. This way, I keep the information fresh in my mind, and it helps me reorient my brain back to what is truly important. On top of that, it helps me gain more knowledge about the market, even though I'm only spending a short amount of time each day on this knowledge-seeking. Try it out and see if it works for you.

As much as building up your knowledge bank is important, it is also essential for you to take action. If all you do is learn, read, and research, then you will never reach the point where you actually move forward and purchase your first investment property. It can be scary because it is such a significant financial commitment, but it is something you need to do if you want to become a successful real estate investor. Trust your instincts and the knowledge you have, and you will do great. Remember to surround yourself with people who are more experienced in this area and seek their advice whenever you need it. This will help you continue to grow and avoid common mistakes that many other investors might have made. It is never a bad idea to expand your circle and network, so make sure you are doing your best to build a strong team.

There are many moving parts when it comes to real estate investing and the BRRRR method. It can seem overwhelming to juggle everything, but once you take one small step and continue taking other small steps afterward, you will see that it is not that difficult. You will start to build momentum, and once you have your first property rented out and leverage that to acquire your second property, you will gain a good understanding of this method and how to use it going forward. You are about to embark on an exciting journey, and I know you will do well. It all begins with a single deliberate step and embracing the process. Remember to stay committed to your goals and let each experience propel you toward financial freedom and lasting success. I sincerely wish you nothing but success and happiness as you start investing in real estate and making your dreams come true.

GLOSSARY

1031 Exchange: This allows for tax to be deferred by selling a property and using that money to buy a new property without paying capital gains tax on the sale.

Appraisal: An estimate of the value of a property provided by a professional.

Appreciation: The increase in the value of a property or another investment over time.

ARV: After-Repair Value, the estimated value of a particular property once renovations are completed.

BRRRR: A real estate investment strategy that stands for Buy, Rehab, Rent, Refinance, and Repeat.

Cash Flow: The income generated from rent after subtracting expenses.

Cash-Out Refinance: A type of refinancing where you take out a new mortgage for more than what you currently owe and pocket the extra cash to use as needed.

Closing Costs: Fees that are due at the end of the property purchase process.

Contractor: A person who is hired to perform repairs and renovations on a property.

Credit Score: A three-digit number that shows how well someone manages debt. Lenders use it to evaluate loan eligibility and determine borrowing terms.

Debt-to-Equity Ratio: A way to measure financial risk by comparing how much debt is owed on a property to how much equity (ownership value) the owner has.

Deed: A document that allows a property to be transferred from one owner to another.

Due Diligence: A period just before finalizing the sale of a property during which an investigation takes place.

Equity: The difference between the market value and the amount owed on the property.

Exit Strategy: The plan for making a profit from a real estate investment without retaining ownership.

Flipping: Buying a property, fixing it up, and selling it again in a short time with the goal of making a profit.

Individual Ownership: When one person owns a property outright, with complete control and full responsibility for it.

Interest Rate: A percentage fee that is charged on a loan.

Leverage: To use a loan or credit to purchase a piece of real estate.

LLC (Limited Liability Company): A business structure that lets you own real estate while protecting your personal assets from potential risks or lawsuits.

LTV: This stands for loan-to-value ratio and is used to calculate the potential risk of a loan compared to the value of the property.

MLS (Multiple Listing Service): A shared database where real estate agents list properties for sale, making it easier for buyers and sellers to connect.

Opportunity Zones: Designated areas that offer tax benefits for real estate investors.

Property Manager: A person who is hired to manage a rental property, including tenants, maintenance, and the general day-to-day operations of the property.

Real Estate Agent: A professional with the necessary licenses to assist with buying and selling properties.

Refinance: A method of recovering your capital on a property by replacing your current loan with another one that potentially offers better terms and interest rates.

ROI: Return on Investment, a percentage or ratio that indicates how profitable an investment is or will be.

REFERENCES

Achen, P. 2025. "2024 Vacation Rental Stats Roundup." Rent Responsibly, March 3. https://www.rentresponsibly.org/2024-vacation-rental-stats-roundup/.

Airbnb. n.d. "Success Stories." Accessed July 3, 2025. https://www.airbnb.co.za/resources/hosting-homes/t/success-stories-27?locale=en&_set_bev_on_new_domain=1750448390_EAZjk5MmEyMmJiMT.

Akins, H. 2024. "Spring Cleaning: What Rental Property Documents to Keep, What to Toss, and When." REI Hub, August 26. https://www.reihub.net/resources/rental-property-document-retention/.

All Property Management. 2024. "Landlord's Guide to Rental Property Accounting." December 12. https://www.allpropertymanagement.com/blog/post/landlord-rental-property-accounting/.

Allred, C. 2025. "How to Choose the Right Real Estate Broker." *Investopedia*, April 29. https://www.investopedia.com/updates/real-estate-broker/.

AmeriMac Appraisal Management. 2024. "Can Your Neighborhood Affect Your Property Appraisal? Key Factors to Consider." August 13. https://www.amerimacmanagement.com/about/blog/can-your-neighborhood-affect-your-property-appraisal-key-factors-to-consider/.

Araj, V. 2024. "House Hacking Incorporates a Variety of Ways You Can Use Your House to Pay Living Expenses. Learn What House Hacking Is and How You Can Make It Work for You." Rocket Mortgage, April 3. https://www.rocketmortgage.com/learn/house-hacking.

ArchEyes Team. 2023. "Home Renovations You Shouldn't DIY: A Guide to Professional Help." ArchEyes, September 24. https://archeyes.com/home-renovations-you-shouldnt-diy-a-guide-to-professional-help/.

Ashton, D. 2024. "What Is the BRRRR Method (and How Does It Work)?" University of the Built Environment, September 9. https://www.ube.ac.uk/whats-happening/articles/what-is-the-brrrr-method/.

Birk, C. 2025. "Complete Guide to the VA Home Loan." Veterans United Home Loans, August 1. https://www.veteransunited.com/va-loans/.

Bitton, D. 2023. "How to Find Tenants: Everything You Need to Know." DoorLoop Hubs, April 3. https://www.doorloop.com/hub/find-tenants.

Blankenship, M. 2023a. "7 BRRRR Method Risks You Should Know Before Investing." Call Porter, October 6. https://callporter.com/blog/brrrr-method-risks/.

Blankenship, M. 2023b. "The BRRRR Method vs. Flix & Flip: What's The Difference?" Call Porter, October 19. https://callporter.com/blog/the-brrrr-method-vs-flix-flip/.

Blankenship, M. 2024a. "5 Common Types of Real Estate Investing Contracts." Call Porter, March 1. https://callporter.com/blog/real-estate-investing-contracts/.

Blankenship, M. 2024b. "7 Real Estate Investing Calculators You Can Use for Free." Call Porter, December 31. https://callporter.com/blog/real-estate-investing-calculators/.

Boldyreff, K. 2020. "House Hacking 101: What It Is and How It Works." Northpointe.com, May 28. https://www.northpointe.com/learn/homes-real-estate/house-hacking-101-what-it-is-and-how-it-works/.

Brock, M. 2024. "What Is a Real Estate Portfolio and How Do You Build a Collection of Real Estate Investments?" Rocket Mortgage, March 27. https://www.rocketmortgage.com/learn/real-estate-portfolio.

Cartier, B. 2024. "Rental Property Accounting & Bookkeeping 101: Landlord's Guide." *Stessa*, December 23. https://www.stessa.com/blog/rental-property-accounting-101/.

Casago. 2024. "What Makes a Good Airbnb Property? A Guide to Amenities, Fees & More." Casago, September 1. https://casago.com/blog/airbnb-property-guide/.

Cepf, L. G. T., and M. Grace. 2025. "Finding the Right Real Estate Agent: Everything You Need to Know." Business Insider, April 11. https://www.businessinsider.com/personal-finance/mortgages/how-to-find-real-estate-agent.

Chen, J. 2024. "Multiple Listing Service (MLS): Definition, Benefits, and Fees." *Investopedia*, July 9. https://www.investopedia.com/terms/m/multiple-listing-service-mls.asp.

Collins, D. 2023. "What Is Wholesale Real Estate? This Guide Will Help You Understand the Basics, How the Selling Process Works, and Best Practices." December 21. https://www.rocketmortgage.com/learn/wholesale-real-estate.

Conde, A. 2023. "What Is a Real Estate Partnership?" SmartAsset, October 20. https://smartasset.com/investing/real-estate-partnership.

Crace, M. 2024. "Hard Money Loans, Unlike Traditional Loans, Are Based on the Collateral That Secures the Loan." Rocket Mortgage, February 22. https://www.rocketmortgage.com/learn/hard-money-loans/.

Dar, S. 2025. "Why Landlords Need a Separate Bank Account for Rental Property." Baselane, May 28. https://www.baselane.com/resources/separate-bank-account-for-rental-property/.

Davis, M. 2025a. "How to Find Your Return on Investment (ROI) in Real Estate." *Investopedia*, June 1. https://www.investopedia.com/articles/basics/11/calculate-roi-real-estate-investments.asp.

Davis, M. 2025b. "Real Estate Agent vs. Mortgage Broker: What's the Difference?" *Investopedia*, March 14. https://www.investopedia.com/articles/financialca reers/10/real-estate-agent-mortgage-broker.asp.

Dehan, A. 2025. "Hard Money Lending: Guide to Hard Money Loans." *Bankrate*, February 28. https://www.bankrate.com/mortgages/hard-money-lenders/.

Dixon, A. 2025. "Determining How Much You Should Charge for Rent." Smart Asset, January 30. Accessed July 12. https://smartasset.com/mortgage/how-much-you-should-charge-for-rent.

Dodge, A. 2025. "What Does Off-Market Mean in Real Estate?" FastExpert, April 25. https://www.fastexpert.com/blog/what-does-off-market-mean/.

DoorLoop. n.d. "The 2023 BRRRR Method Ultimate Guide for Real Estate Investors." Accessed July 8. https://www.doorloop.com/hubs/brrrr.

Dossey, J. 2023a. "4 Best Strategies to BRRRR Deals with No Money." Call Porter, October 12. https://callporter.com/blog/brrrr-method-with-no-money/.

Dossey, J. 2023b. "Investing in Real Estate: 7 Steps to Your First Deal." Call Porter, May 11. https://callporter.com/blog/guide-to-investing-in-real-estate/.

Drake Law. 2025. "Key Legal Factors to Consider Before Investing in Real Estate." June 16. https://www.drakelaw.ca/legal-insights/key-legal-factors-to-consider-before-investing-in-real-estate.

Duncan, A. 2024. "Staying Motivated in a Tough Market." Agent Monday, December 23. https://www.agentmonday.com/how-to-stay-motivated-in-a-tough-market/.

Evans, K. 2024. "Understanding Off-Market Listings: A Strategic Tool for Real Estate Agents." *Luxury Presence*, August 13. https://www.luxurypresence.com/blogs/off-market-listings/.

Fairless, J. 2022. "Real Estate Horror Stories from Five Active Investors." Best Ever Commercial Real Estate, June 9. https://www.bestevercre.com/blog/real-estate-horror-stories-five-active-investors.

Fraraccio, M. 2025. "Buying an Existing Business? How to Finance Your Purchase." CO—by US Chamber of Commerce, January 31. https://www.uschamber.com/co/run/business-financing/financing-buying-an-existing-business.

Freitas, T. 2025. "What Is an FHA Loan?" *Bankrate*, May 9. https://www.bankrate.com/mortgages/what-is-an-fha-loan/.

Gibson, J. 2025. "Factors to Consider Before You Refinance Your Mortgage." *Investopedia*, March 24. https://www.investopedia.com/mortgage/refinance/9-things-to-know-before-you-refinance-mortgage/.

The Ginther Group. 2024. "Setting Real Estate Goals: Buying, Selling, or Investing." December 23. https://theginthergroup.com/tips/buying-selling-investing-goals/.

Goade, C. 2023. "Is a Stack of Cash Better than Slow but Steady Returns? A Look at Flipping and the BRRRR Method." BiggerPockets, November 5. https://www.biggerpockets.com/blog/flip-vs-brrrr-real-estate.

Goff, K. 2023. "What Is the 70% Rule in House Flipping?" *Bankrate*, February 21. https://www.bankrate.com/real-estate/70-percent-rule-house-flipping/.

Grace, M., and A. J. Yale. 2025. "Understanding the Loan-to-Value Ratio (LTV) and What It Means for Mortgage Borrowers." Business Insider, March 28. https://www.businessinsider.com/personal-finance/mortgages/loan-to-value-ratio-mortgage-refinancing.

Graham, K. 2024. "An FHA Loan Is a Government-Backed Loan That Allows You to Buy a Home with Less Strict Financial Requirements." Rocket Mortgage, November 20. https://www.rocketmortgage.com/learn/fha-loans.

Gratton, P. 2025a. "Flipping Houses: How It Works, Where to Start, and 5 Mistakes to Avoid." *Investopedia*, February 6. https://www.investopedia.com/articles/mortgages-real-estate/08/house-flip.asp.

Gratton, P. 2025b. "What Is Depreciation Recapture?" *Investopedia*, February 25. https://www.investopedia.com/terms/d/depreciationrecapture.asp

Harris, V. 2019. "How to Get Started in Real Estate Investing: Your 90 Day Plan." Mashvisor Real Estate, January 17. https://www.mashvisor.com/blog/get-started-real-estate-investing-90-day-plan/.

Hayes, A. 2024. "Loan-to-Value (LTV) Ratio: What It Is, How to Calculate, Example." *Investopedia*, September 26. https://www.investopedia.com/terms/l/loantovalue.asp.

Heath, K. 2024. "Lender or Realtor: Who Should You Talk to First Before Buying a House? FastExpert, March 13. https://www.fastexpert.com/blog/lender-or-realtor-who-to-talk-first-before-buying-house/.

Hendricks, M. 2023. "How Private Money Lending Works." SmartAsset, March 19. https://smartasset.com/personal-loans/how-private-money-lending-works.

Henson, T. 2024. "Flipping vs. Renting—Which Real Estate Strategy Is Best for Long-term Gains." Beach Front Property Management Inc., December 18. https://bfpminc.com/flipping-vs-renting-which-real-estate-strategy-is-best-for-long-term-gains/.

Hrovat, J. 2024. "Maximizing Short-Term Rental with the BRRRR Method." UpRev, October 15. https://www.uprev.co/post/maximizing-short-term-rental-brrrr-method.

Huff, J. 2023. "BRRRR vs. Flipping: A Comparison of Real Estate Investment Strategies." Jacobs & Co. Real Estate, November 8. https://www.jacobsandco.com/blog/brrrr-vs-flipping-a-comparison-of-real-estate-investment-strategies/.

Hughes, E. 2025. "Completing My First BRRRR Property." Rental Income Advisors, April 28. https://www.rentalincomeadvisors.com/blog/my-first-brrrr-property.

Internal Revenue Service. n.d. "Tips on Rental Real Estate Income, Deductions and Recordkeeping." Accessed July 14. https://www.irs.gov/businesses/small-businesses-self-employed/tips-on-rental-real-estate-income-deductions-and-recordkeeping.

Internal Revenue Service. 2024. "Publication 527: Residential Rental Property." https://www.irs.gov/publications/p527.

The Investopedia Team. 2023. "4 Tips for Joining an Investment Club." *Investopedia*, September 16. https://www.investopedia.com/articles/01/062001.asp.

Jamal, A. 2021. "How to Diversify Your Real Estate Portfolio." *Forbes*, August 3. https://www.forbes.com/sites/forbesbooksauthors/2021/08/03/how-to-diversify-your-real-estate-portfolio/.

Johnson, M. 2023. "6 Renovation Projects That Pay Off for ROI, According to an Expert." *Architectural Digest*, September 25. https://www.architecturaldigest.com/story/renovation-projects-and-their-roi-according-to-an-expert.

Jones, R. n.d. "Setting Effective Property Investment Goals: How to Achieve Success in 2025." Property Investments UK. https://www.propertyinvestmentsuk.co.uk/5-steps-property-success-goal-setting/.

J. P. Morgan Chase. 2023. "How to Use the BRRRR Method in Real Estate." March 31. https://www.chase.com/personal/mortgage/education/buying-a-home/brrrr-method.

Kagan, J. 2021. "VA Loan: Definition, Eligibility Requirements, Types & Terms." *Investopedia*, November 27. https://www.investopedia.com/terms/v/valoan.asp.

Karani, A. 2020. "How to Evaluate a Neighborhood Before Investing." Mashvisor Real Estate, December 27. https://www.mashvisor.com/blog/evaluate-a-neighborhood-investing/.

Knaack, E. 2024. "Building a Successful REI Team & Keeping Them Accountable." *Deal Machine* (blog), May 16. https://www.dealmachine.com/blog/how-to-build-a-team.

Kopp, C. M. 2020. "1% Rule in Real Estate: What It Is, How It Works, Examples." *Investopedia*, November 11. https://www.investopedia.com/terms/o/one-percent-rule.asp.

Langager, C. 2025. "Reducing or Avoiding Capital Gains Tax on Home Sales." *Investopedia*, February 23. https://www.investopedia.com/ask/answers/06/capitalgainhomesale.asp.

Lecko, D. 2021. "What Is ARV in Real Estate & How to Calculate." *Deal Machine* (blog), December 23. https://www.dealmachine.com/blog/what-is-arv-in-real-estate.

Lombardo, T. 2024. "Maximizing Returns: The Power of Evaluating Neighborhoods for Residential Real Estate Investment Success." Carolina Venture REI, February 5. https://carolinaventurerei.com/evaluating-neighbor hoods-for-residential-real-estate-investment-success/.

Lubin, D. 2023. "3 Types of Loans to Maximize the BRRRR Method." Kiavi Funding, Inc., December 15. https://www.kiavi.com/blog/three-types-of-loans-to-maximize-the-brrrr-method.

Lubin, D. 2024. "How to Calculate a Profitable BRRRR Property." Kiavi Funding, Inc., March 25. https://www.kiavi.com/blog/how-to-calculate-a-profitable-brrrr-property.

The Luxury Playbook. 2025. "10 Best Real Estate Investment Exit Strategies (+ Examples)." April 17. https://theluxuryplaybook.com/real-estate-investment-exit-strategies/.

Maldonado, J. D. 2022. "What's the Story of Your First Deal?" BiggerPockets, June 22. https://www.biggerpockets.com/forums/48/topics/1046282-whats-the-story-of-your-first-deal.

Martin, E. J. 2025. "What Is a Private Mortgage Lender?" *Bankrate*, March 10. https://www.bankrate.com/mortgages/what-is-a-private-mortgage-lender/.

Moeen, A. 2024. "ARV Calculator—After Repair Value." Omni Calculator, April 23. https://www.omnicalculator.com/finance/arv

Moore, A. 2024. "Case Study: A Real Estate Success Story with Hard Money Funding." Lending Bee, May 13. https://lendingbeeinc.com/blog/case-study-a-real-estate-success-story-with-hard-money-funding.

myRealPage. 2025. "Why Reinvesting in Your Real Estate Business Is Essential and How to Do It." myRealPage, May 5. https://myrealpage.com/real-estate-market ing/reinvesting-real-estate-business-essential/.

National Association of Realtors. 2024. "Highlights from the Profile of Home Buyers and Sellers." November 4. https://www.nar.realtor/research-and-statistics/research-reports/highlights-from-the-profile-of-home-buyers-and-sellers.

National Association of Realtors. 2025. "Remodeling Impact." April 9. https://www.nar.realtor/research-and-statistics/research-reports/remodeling-impact.

Nesbit, J. 2025. "What Is the 70% Rule in House Flipping and Does It Show How Much to Pay for a Distressed Property?" Rocket Mortgage, February 19. https://www.rocketmortgage.com/learn/what-is-70-rule-in-house-flipping.

Nichols, B. 2023. "Mastering BRRRR: The Power of Refinancing in Real Estate." *Deal Machine* (blog), December 3. https://www.dealmachine.com/blog/master ing-brrrr-refinancing-in-real-estate-investing.

Nicola, G. 2025. "Flipping vs. BRRR: Which Real Estate Investment Strategy Is Right for You?" Tallbox, March 28. https://www.tallboxdesign.com/flipping-vs-brrrr-which-strategy-is-for-you/.

Nock Deighton. n.d. "ROI (Return on Investment) Calculator." Accessed June 29. https://www.nockdeighton.co.uk/investment-calculator.

Nowacki, L. 2024a. "Breaking Down the 1% Rule in Real Estate: What You Should Know Before Investing." Rocket Mortgage, February 27. https://www.rocket mortgage.com/learn/1-rule-real-estate.

Nowacki, L. 2024b. "Understand the BRRRR Method of Real Estate Investments." Rocket Mortgage, May 16. https://www.rocketmortgage.com/learn/brrrr.

Olson, L. n.d. "10 Types of Insurance for Real Estate Investors to Consider." Obie Insurance. Accessed July 2. https://www.obieinsurance.com/blog/insurance-for-real-estate-investors.

Pallardy, C. 2025. "How to Find and Buy Off-Market Homes." *Investopedia*, March 17. https://www.investopedia.com/articles/personal-finance/121415/how-find-and-buy-offmarket-homes.asp.

Paquette, A. 2019. "Success Story of the Week: Will FHA work for you?" *Athena Paquette* (blog), August 8. https://athenapaquette.com/success-story-of-the-week-will-fha-work-for-you/.

Parker, T. 2025. "Home Improvements That Require Permits." *Investopedia*, April 17. https://www.investopedia.com/financial-edge/1012/home-improvements-that-require-permits.aspx.

Peterson, L. 2025. "How many hours per week does it take to manage a successful Airbnb?" L'abode Accommodation, April 21. https://labodeaccommodation.com.au/time-spent-on-an-airbnb/.

Pisano, N. 2024. "Residential Real Estate Investing in 2024: More Rent Money, More Rental Problems." Clever, July 22. https://listwithclever.com/research/residential-real-estate-investing-2024/.

Plati, A. 2024. "How to Conduct a Real Estate Market Study: The Perfect Guide." October 21. https://www.netquest.com/en/blog/how-to-conduct-real-estate-market-study-perfect-guide.

Ramsey Solutions. 2025. "How to Create a Home Renovation Budget." March 27. https://www.ramseysolutions.com/real-estate/home-renovation-budget?srsltid=AfmBOorAz3wQZNv1mvhEhlIaFeKSAP-z-S5H9BlBA5AMzkdS0Ifp YAbS.

Reiff, N. 2025. "Do-It-Yourself Projects to Boost Home Value." *Investopedia*, March 18. https://www.investopedia.com/articles/mortgages-real-estate/08/diy-home-projects.asp.

Rodriguez, C. 2024. "To Flip or to BRRRR?" BiggerPockets, March 9. https://www.biggerpockets.com/forums/48/topics/1127968-to-flip-or-to-brrrr.

Rogers, E. 2025. "What You Need to Know About Building Wealth with the BRRRR Method in St. George." Red Rock Real Estate, February 3. https://www.relocate tosunnystgeorge.com/blog/what-you-need-to-know-about-building-wealth-with-the-brrrr-method-in-st-george.

Rosenberg, E. 2025. "Ultimate Guide to BRRRR Method For Real Estate Investment." Baselane, May 14. https://www.baselane.com/resources/brrrr-method-for-real-estate/.

Segal, T. 2024. "Hard Money Loan: Definition, Uses, and Pros & Cons." *Investopedia*, May 7. https://www.investopedia.com/terms/h/hard_money_loan.asp.

Segal, T. 2025. "Federal Housing Administration (FHA) Loan: Requirements, Limits, How to Qualify." *Investopedia*, March 27. https://www.investopedia.com/terms/f/fhaloan.asp.

Shehaj, E. 2022. "The Ultimate 60-Day Action Plan for the Paralyzed Newbie Longing for a First Deal." BiggerPockets, July 29. https://www.biggerpockets.com/blog/60-day-newbie-action-plan.

Shour, E. 2025. "Should You Hire a Property Manager? The Pros & Cons." Stessa, April 15. https://www.stessa.com/blog/should-you-hire-property-manager/.

Shugrue, D. 2023. "How to Plan Your Home Renovation Costs." *Budget Dumpster* (blog), December 4. https://www.budgetdumpster.com/blog/budget-home-renovation.

Sprenkle, B. 2024. "The Dilemma on Whether to Refinance or Sell." American Apartment Owners Association, June 4. https://american-apartment-owners-association.org/property-management/the-dilemma-on-whether-to-refinance-or-sell/?srsltid=AfmBOorvn4BfX0OGOJGafoPelEyfNera-1-FN3rAl WXGI5QpqvG5EAxY.

Stammers, R. 2021. "Should You Buy and Hold Real Estate or Flip Properties?" *Investopedia*, January 27. https://www.investopedia.com/articles/mortgages-real-estate/08/flipping-flip-properties.asp

Stohler, N. 2024. "How to Find Off-Market Properties: 13 Winning Methods." Azibo, June 28. https://www.azibo.com/blog/how-to-find-off-market-proper ties.

Subel, M. 2024. "Home Remodeling Steps: A Checklist to Help Plan and Organize Your Renovation." Dave Fox, August 29. https://www.davefox.com/resource-center/whole-home-remodeling-steps-checklist.

Talbot, A. 2025. "What Is 'House Hacking' and How Is It Helping Millennials and Gen Z Buy Houses?" Webster First Federal Credit Union, January 22. https://www.websterfirst.com/blog/what-is-house-hacking-definition/.

Travelers. 2023. "10 Common Rental Property Repairs Landlords Need to Know About." February 28. https://www.travelers.com/resources/home/landlords/10-common-rental-property-repairs-landlords-need-to-know-about.

Turner, B. 2020. "The BRRRR Origin Story: How I Discovered This Amazing—No Money—Real Estate Strategy." BiggerPockets, July 11. https://www.biggerpock ets.com/blog/brrrr-origin-story.

Vazquez, J. 2024. "The Difference Between Rehabbing a Flip, Short-Term Rental, Corporate Rental, Long-Term Rental, and BRRRR Strategy." Graystone Investment Group, August 30. https://graystoneig.com/articles/the-difference-between-rehabbing-a-flip-short-term-rental-corporate-rental-long-term-rental-and-brrrr-strategy.

Villegas, F. 2024. "Real Estate Market Analysis: What It Is & How to Do It." QuestionPro, April 10. https://www.questionpro.com/blog/real-estate-market-analysis/.

Wall Street Prep. 2024. "After-Repair Value (ARV)." February 20. https://www.wall streetprep.com/knowledge/after-repair-value-arv/.

Webber, M. R. 2024. "The Top Renovations That Increase Home Value in 2024." *Bankrate*, May 13. https://www.bankrate.com/homeownership/home-renova tions-that-return-the-most-at-resale/.

Welty, S. 2025. "Short-Term Rental vs. Long-Term Rental: 12 Things to Know." Good Life Property Management, May 19. https://www.goodlifemgmt.com/blog/short-term-rental-vs-long-term-rental/.

White, J. 2025. "What's a Good Return on Investment (ROI)?" SmartAsset, May 28. https://smartasset.com/investing/whats-a-good-return-on-investment-roi.

White, M., and A. Conde. 2024. "How to Start Wholesaling Real Estate in 7 Steps." Smart Asset, July 29. https://smartasset.com/mortgage/how-to-get-started-wholesaling-real-estate.

Williams, T. 2022. "Look for these 12 red flags to avoid hiring bad contractors." Architectural Digest, March 14. https://www.architecturaldigest.com/story/bad-contractors-red-flags-warning-signs.

Wood, R. W. 2024. "What Is a 1031 Exchange? Know the Rules." *Investopedia*, December 16. https://www.investopedia.com/financial-edge/0110/10-things-to-know-about-1031-exchanges.aspx.

Woodman, C. 2023. "How to Scale Your Real Estate Portfolio." New Silver, May 24. https://newsilver.com/the-lender/how-to-scale-your-real-estate-portfolio/.

Woodman, C. 2025. "Over Leveraged Real Estate—What Is It and How to Avoid It." New Silver, March 24. https://newsilver.com/the-lender/over-leveraged-real-estate/.

Woodward, E. 2024. "The BRRRR Method: What It Means and What It Stands For." *Bankrate*, February 23. https://www.bankrate.com/real-estate/brrrr-method-in-real-estate/.

Young Entrepreneur Council. 2023. "How Real Estate Investors Can Find Off-Market Properties." *Forbes*, February 14. https://www.forbes.com/councils/theyec/2023/02/14/how-real-estate-investors-can-find-off-market-properties/.

Zinn, D. 2024. "How to Flip a House: A Beginner's Guide." *Bankrate*, July 8. https://www.bankrate.com/real-estate/flipping-houses/.

IMAGE REFERENCES

Anke, Peggy. 2018. *Airbnb*. Image. Pixabay. May 19. https://pixabay.com/photos/airbnb-air-bnb-apartment-3399753/.

Cytonn Photography. 2018. *Two People Shaking Hands*. Image. Unsplash. March 23. https://unsplash.com/photos/two-people-shaking-hands-n95VMLxqM2I.

Danilyuk, Pavel. 2021. *Couple Holding Blueprint of a House*. Image. Pexels. May 18. https://www.pexels.com/photo/couple-holding-blueprint-of-a-house-7937668/

Kindel Media. 2021. *People Holding a Key*. Image. Pexels. April 16. https://www.pexels.com/photo/people-holding-a-key-7579192/.

Lehner, Stefan. 2021. *A Room That Has Some Tools in It*. Image. Unsplash. October 18. https://unsplash.com/photos/a-room-that-has-some-tools-in-it-biRt6RXejuk.

McBee, David. 2018. *High Angle Shot of Suburban Neighborhood*. Image. Pexels. October 28. https://www.pexels.com/photo/high-angle-shot-of-suburban-neighborhood-1546168/.

Mils, Alexander. 2019. *Fan of 100 U. S. Dollar Banknotes*. Image. Unsplash. March 27. https://unsplash.com/photos/fan-of-100-us-dollar-banknotes-lCPhGxs7pww.

RDNE Stock Project. 2021. *Person Wearing Silver Ring Holding Red Pen on White Printer Paper*. Image. Pexels. May 25. https://www.pexels.com/photo/person-wearing-silver-ring-holding-red-pen-on-white-printer-paper-8052843/

Thirdman. 2021. *Shallow Focus Photo of a Realtor Posting a Sold Sticker*. Image. Pexels. June 24. https://www.pexels.com/photo/shallow-focus-photo-of-a-realtor-posting-a-sold-sticker-8470803/.

Struggling to figure out how to make money in real estate without losing your sanity and savings? This is the ultimate guide designed just for beginners, simplifying every step toward financial freedom with rental properties!

Did you know that over **90% of the world's millionaires earned their fortune by investing in real estate**?

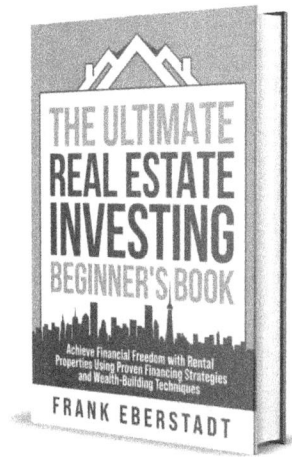

In truth, real estate generates more money than all industrial investments combined.

But how do you get started? What types of properties should you invest in? How can you finance your investments without the risk of losing all your hard-earned money?

This **wealth-building guide** provides the answers you seek while laying out a 3-step blueprint to help you live the dream life through real estate.

Inside, you will discover:

- **Beginner-friendly ways to start earning income through the Build-Master-Profit framework**
- A closer look at the **different types of real estate investments** – from single-family homes to commercial properties
- Important **key metrics**, such as cash flow, NOI, and cap rate to evaluate and compare properties accurately
- **Step-by-step property evaluation and risk assessment** with practical tips and formulas
- How to navigate taxes and legalities to maximize your returns and protect your investments
- The lucrative world of short-term rentals with Airbnb, including setup tips, management advice, and how to leverage this platform for maximum profit
- Interactive elements to help you apply your newfound knowledge and build confidence

And much more!

This book breaks down every concept into **simple, actionable steps**, to ensure you'll confidently build your real estate empire. The path to financial freedom is closer than you think.

Invest smartly, effectively, and SUCCESSFULLY.

Scan the QR code below and get your copy now.

How to launch your own Airbnb empire from scratch — no property management experience required.

Data from Stratos Jet Charters show that **approximately 14,000 new hosts are joining Airbnb... *every month.***

So if you plan on turning a decent profit with your Airbnb listing, you will have to find creative ways to stand out from the competition.

The good news is there's nothing to worry about.

Because the truth is anyone can start their own Airbnb rental business.

All you need are **practical strategies and principles that have been proven to work repeatedly.**

In this book, you'll discover:

- The simple **6-step framework for launching an Airbnb listing from scratch**
- The 4 primary types of Airbnb accommodations and which one you should use for your property
- How to calculate the profitability of your Airbnb listing — always look at these 5 factors
- **Airbnb Insurance: what's included and what additional coverage you might need**
- The 7 best safety tips for Airbnb hosts
- **The subtle difference between a house manual and house rules**

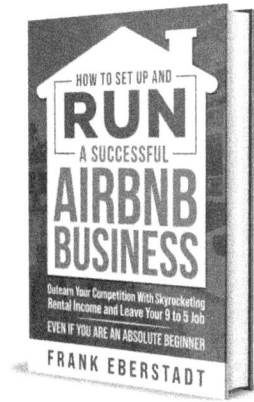

- **3 core components of any effective Airbnb listing —** focus on THIS element above all others
- How to automate these behind-the-scenes processes for your Airbnb business
- **9 signs that starting your own short-term rental business is the perfect fit for you**

And much more!

There's no secret "hack" to winning on Airbnb.

And unlike other guides that promote overly complex strategies filled with technical terminology… this book is designed specifically for *anyone* to understand.

So whether you're already an Airbnb host or have just discovered how Airbnb works, you'll have all the fundamental knowledge you need to start earning rental income on the side.

Scan the QR code below and get your copy now.

Unlock the secrets to skyrocketing your rental income and bookings with this comprehensive guide to mastering Airbnb!

Your Airbnb property isn't just bricks and mortar—it's a treasure chest of untapped potential. If you only had the right map to guide you, imagine the possibilities.

You could unlock your property's full potential, transform your Airbnb business into a consistent income generator, and finally leave behind the days of just scraping by.

This is where Frank Eberstadt steps in.

He's back with his latest book that promises to be the companion that steers you beyond Airbnb basics and puts you confidently in the driver's seat.

Inside, you will discover:

- **How to research your market effectively and outsmart your competition** – identify your unique selling proposition and elevate your Airbnb above the competition!
- **An arsenal of advanced pricing strategies tailored for different seasons and property types** – navigate the tumultuous tides of seasonal demands and make sure your rental rates are always on point
- **The magic of transitioning and diversification to ensure consistent income** – you no longer need to worry about slow seasons

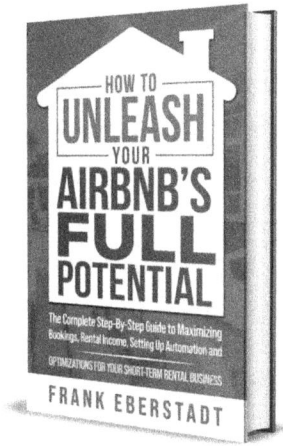

- **The power of data analytics and metrics to make informed business decisions** – drive informed decisions to boost your income
- **Tips and tricks to optimize your Airbnb listing and attract more bookings** – make your listing so appealing that guests can't resist clicking "book now"!
- **Secrets to building a stellar reputation and becoming a beloved Superhost** – charm your guests and earn glowing 5-star reviews with ease!
- **Techniques to automate your Airbnb business and save valuable time** – imagine spending less time on admin and more time enjoying the fruits of your success

And much more!

Wave goodbye to frustration and uncertainty – step into a future where your Airbnb investment transforms into a consistent income-generating machine!

It is time to up your Airbnb game.

Scan the QR code below and get your copy now.

ABOUT THE AUTHOR

Frank Eberstadt is an accommodation manager and bestselling author of books on Airbnb and real estate investing.

His books address property management and business growth in short-term rentals, guiding readers to seek and capitalize on opportunities in the market while nurturing successful businesses along the way.

Frank is the accommodation manager for an investment group operating hotels and motels in Australia. He has established his own successful Airbnb business, and has grown his portfolio to six properties. Frank began his first Airbnb business from the ground up and knows how hard it can be to break into property listings and attract guests. Using his extensive experience in the accommodation industry, his aim is to lay out a clear, step-by-step path that even complete newbies can follow to success.

Frank's interest in vacation property stems from his many years traveling as a solo backpacker, something he now does with his family. These two very different traveling experiences have fed into his awareness of what makes a successful vacation rental, and have been key to his success as an Airbnb business owner.

Frank still loves to travel, and enjoys surfing, but more than anything, he loves to spend quality time with his family, no matter where their adventures take them.